China Strategies in the Belt and Road Initiative

Dr. Paul Eberle

and

Dr. Arthur H Tafero

Contents

Forward

The strategies that will be discussed in this book are both factual and theoretical. Some are factual with substantiated data from China's own publications, such as the *China Daily* newspaper and announcements on *CGTN* (China Global Television Network), the national television station of China. Both of these media are under strict guidelines provided by Xinhua News Agency, the watchdog of the Communist Party of China in Beijing for Chinese media.

Other data in this book is conjecture, but highly substantiated conjecture, based on current Chinese expenditures, location of China's military base (they only have one), and other meaningful variables and negotiations by China. We would also like to thank the over 400 Chinese business professionals and educators who provided information and assistance for this text.

Some of the scenarios presented in this book could be of concern to both China and the world, if negotiations with Russia are not handled properly. Russia is a competitor of Saudi Arabia for selling oil in the EU; China is a partner of Saudi Arabia in the Maritime Belt and Road. This is a problem for all three countries. Russia will not likely stand by while they lose market share in oil sales to China in the EU, especially in Germany.

If China fails to keep Russia happy, and does not include them immediately in Belt and Road activities and profits, Vladimir Putin will not be very patient. He will make his own Belt and Road plans; and if it includes the United States, it will greatly reduce the effectiveness of China in the Belt and Road, or even virtually destroy the Chinese Belt and Road's effectiveness.

A combination of the US, Russia, Japan, India and South Korea (all countries out of the Maritime Route) would most likely reduce the Chinese Belt and Road efforts to a minor role. But that is only one dreadful scenario for China; there are many positive ones as well. We will examine all of them, and China's CPC will ultimately make the final decisions as to what directions they will go in, what strategies they will employ, and what gambles they are willing to take. It should be an interesting economic development for several countries over the next decade.

Paul Eberle, Phd
Arthur H Tafero, Phd

Chapter One

General Chinese Strategies for the Belt and Road Initiative: The CPC in Beijing and Factional Differences

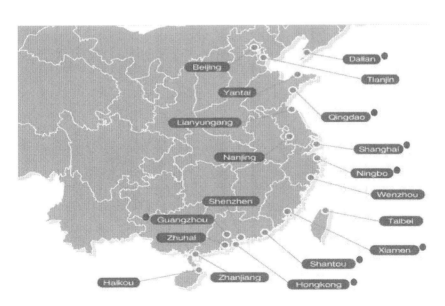

Ports in SW China Will Be Starting Points for Maritime Route

https://www.solent.ac.uk/image-library/research/ports-in-china.jpg

China currently has three major plans for routes along the Belt and Road. These plans are alternately called One Belt, One Road, The Belt and Road Initiative, or just plain Belt and Road. The acronyms are logically OBOR and BRI, respectively. For the purpose of brevity, we will refer to these plans as BRI.

There are three schemes within the most recent form of BRI; The Maritime Route, The Southern Overland Route, and the Northern Overland Route. Each of these schemes has a unique set of partners and strategies. They also have varying levels of support within CPC factions located in Beijing.

Like every other political party in the history of mankind, the CPC has two basic factions: the Conservative element of the CPC, which advocates slow changes to the economy and strong political controls, while maintaining strict adherence to Communist and Socialist principles. However, they are open to the idea of making more money for China and the CPC.

The other faction in Beijing is the Liberal element of the CPC, which advocates new and sometimes risky changes to the economy (no risk, no reward). This faction is more in line with the Deng Xiaoping theory of one party, two systems, and an emphasis on rapid economic development. They still employ a Socialist model, but with much more liberalization of economic factors. Getting rich is ok under this model; but not under the Conservative model.

Naturally, modern Chinese businessmen prefer the Liberal model, as it affords them more opportunity to make great profits. However, these same businessmen are constantly aware of the need to pose as companies that promote the Socialist and Communistic models as well. The smart companies play both sides of the fence. Let us examine each of the basic BRI schemes, and how the CPC factions feel about each of them in relationship to the Chinese economy and political control factors.

The Maritime Route

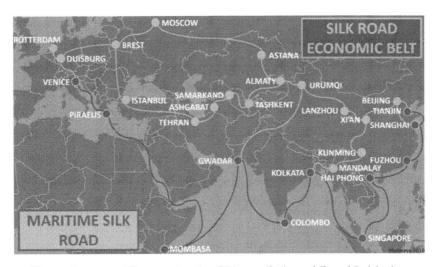

Three Proposed Routes for the Chinese Belt and Road Initiative

https://cdn.techinasia.com/wp-content/uploads/2017/03/Fig1Kai.jpg

At this point in time, the Maritime Route of the BRI is the most important route of the three proposed routes. It is also the one that needs the least infrastructure additions, which translates to the lowest investment by China of any of the three routes. In terms of time, it is already available, and will take very little time to put into effect. Several factors of the Maritime Route have already been put into motion, and China is already profiting from this plan.

The origin of the Maritime Route in China has several points; it could originate in Tianjin, Shanghai, Ningbo, Fuzhou, Xiamen, Quanzhou, Guangzhou, Hainan, Macau, or Hong Kong. Hong Kong has the most international assets of all of these ports, but it is also the most expensive of all Chinese ports to do business in. Renting offices, boat docking, storage and other variables associated with the Maritime Route will be much more expensive than all of the other cities mentioned above. Despite the expense, several Chinese companies will still prefer Hong Kong for a number of reasons.

First and foremost, Hong Kong has a good location. Hong Kong is one of the Westernmost ports with a large city in China. This is both an asset and a liability. Space here is very expensive. it is the close to Ho Chi Minh City, the first main stop along the Maritime Route, but not as close as Hainan. That is why Xi Jinping made an enormous deal with Hainan. Docking ships and storage will be much cheaper there than in Hong Kong, and it is closer to the beginning of the international waters of the Maritime route than any other part of China. Hainan is also more trusted as part of mainland China than is Hong Kong, and Beijing always loves to control projects close to 100% whenever possible..

Hong Kong has over 200 years of experience in both banking and insurance, and the entire business community speaks fluent English, the language of international monetary exchange. These are all considerable assets and may be worth the additional expense. But for those companies looking to cut corners and save money, Hainan will be a more attractive option.

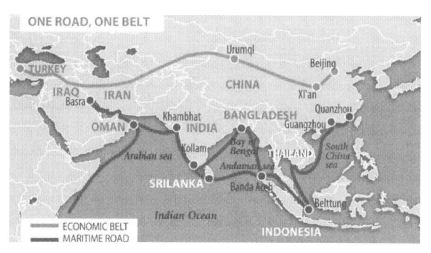

Belt and Road Route Departing From Guangzhou

http://bruce-humes.com/archives/9692

Here is another hopeful version of the Maritime Route. This one bypasses both Hong Kong and Hainan in favor of Guangzhou. This map is obviously created by someone who favors Guangzhou over Hong Kong or Hainan. Every city in Southwest China will have their own map for the Belt and Road, highlighting their city as a departure point. Included in the candidate list would be Hong Kong, Hainan, Macau, Guangzhou, Quanzhou, Xiamen and Fuzhou. Who will be the winner or primary port is still a matter of conjecture.

By last count, there are over 100 suggested maps for the Belt and Road Initiative and its three main routes. That's a lot of maps for only three routes. And there is a lot of wishful thinking in most of these maps. Each city likes to imagine they will be in the thick of things, but in reality, very few cities will be primary ports for the Belt and Road. This map, for instance, doesn't even have China going up the Red Sea to get Arabian oil. That would mean the Chinese would have built the Dibouti military base for nothing. That is highly unlikely.

Next Stop: Vietnam

There was a time when those words would be a bit frightening for some people; especially for American soldiers being shipped out to Vietnam. But these days, Vietnam is a place of economic opportunity, not a war zone.

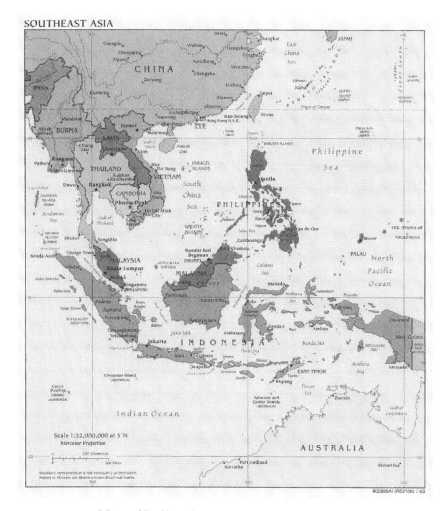

SOUTHEAST ASIA

Map of Indian Ocean and South China Sea

https://aseanup.com/free-maps-asean-countries/

   As you can see from the above map, the most likely first port of call for Chinese ship leaving China would be Viet Nam. A stop could be made either at Haiphong or at Ho Chi Minh City. Both of these Vietnamese cities would be enormous conduits for goods arriving from Laos, Cambodia, Thailand and Myanmar. Even Chinese goods shipped from Kunming could be arriving at these ports as well by train.

Viet Nam has a long international history of dealing with France and the United States in the West. It is the most Westernized of all the Southeast Asian countries, and provides a stopping point before departing for the crossing to Sri Lanka going by Singapore and Indonesia, the next most likely stops on the Maritime Route.

Chinese businessmen are famous for finding the shortest, least expensive and most efficient way of trading in the South China Sea. Only cities directly on the way to the EU via the Maritime Route will be destinations for these Chinese ships.

After leaving Viet Nam, the next likely stop is Singapore, where there is a very old tradition of trade with the West. There is also excellent banking, insurance and oil refinery resources in Singapore; all major considerations for Chinese boat owners. Singapore is one of the most centrally located countries in Asia; they are the Switzerland of Asia. From Singapore, it is almost a straight line to Sri Lanka.

Sri Lanka presents a problem for China and India. India wants China to stop at Calcutta or Madras. Chinese ships might stop at Madras, but it will tack on some extra time and money to the cost of the trip. That will be up to the Chinese business owners. Some owners will send their ships directly to Djibouti from Singapore, others will stop at either Madras or Sri Lanka, but most likely not both. India will primarily be left out of the Belt and Road, if the only stop for Chinese ships is Sri Lanka.

Some Chinese ships will leave Tianjin with nothing on board except the crew, and they will pick up nothing until they get to Saudi Arabia, where they will completely load up with Arabian oil. They will then proceed up the Red Sea to the Suez Canal, and head right for Venice or Florence in Italy, where they will load Italian bullet trains with their oil bound for Germany. In exchange, Germany will send China money electronically, in addition to several hundred luxury German cars, or any combination thereof. These ships will then return to the Red Sea and pick up even more Arab oil on the way back to China.

There is only one problem with this scenario, which we will discuss later in the chapter dealing with countries that are left out of the Belt and Road Initiative. Saudi Arabia is a rival of Russia for selling oil to Germany and the EU. China must be very careful with their dealings with both countries; especially Russia.

Welcome to Africa and the Mideast

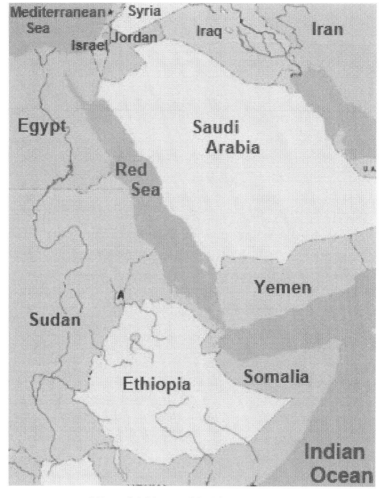

Map of Africa and Mideast Passage

https://www.coral-reef-info.com/red-sea-coral-reefs.html

From Sri Lanka, Chinese ships will make a beeline for Djibouti, but they must be careful to hug the Northern Coast of the Mideast and avoid the coast of Somalia on their way to their lone military base. Of course, Chinese ships using the strategy of carrying nothing until they get to Saudi Arabia will have nothing on board to steal. Coming back, however, will be another story.; those Chinese ships will have to hug the Northern Coast of the Mideast all the way from Saudi Arabia to Sri Lanka.

The map you see above is highly unlikely, a Southern trip to Nairobi will be long and costly, as well as unnecessary. Goods from this part of Africa can easily be shipped by train to Djibouti, and save several days and thousands of dollars for Chinese ships. Trips from Sri Lanka will most likely go directly to Djibouti.

After taking a rest and refueling at Djibouti, Chinese ships will safely be able to go up the Red Sea to the Suez Canal and then to one of three destinations: Italy, Greece, or Turkey. Ships to Italy will be for the German trade, primarily. Trips to Greece will be for the Eastern European Trade; especially for Chinese sneakers and clothes. Trips to Turkey will be primarily made to please the Russians, who will be trading with the Eastern Orthodox Church members of Turkey. Both countries have a substantial population of Eastern Orthodox members who are in close contact with each other.

The Turkish and Greek destinations will primarily be for sneakers and clothes, while the Italy-German destinations will be oil and car oriented. China must keep Russia happy in any of these arrangements. On the way back from these European destinations, Chinese ships will most likely either pick up oil from Saudi Arabia, or goods all along the Maritime Route in exchange for Chinese goods. Oil coming back from Arabia can be refined in Singapore, the most advanced refinery in Asia.

The Return Trip

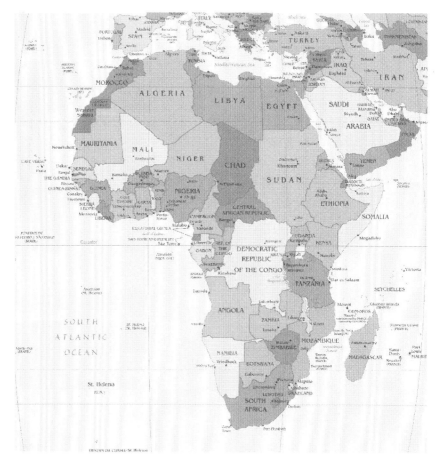

Map of Africa

http://www.travelswithtwo.com/africa-travel-resources/

As we can see from the map above, China will have several options for delivery of ship contents on the way back from the EU and Eastern Europe. There are potential stops in Egypt, Sudan, Eretria, Ethiopia, and other East African countries all the way down to South Africa. And there will be even more opportunities if they decide not to go South at Djibouti.

East Asia and Oceania

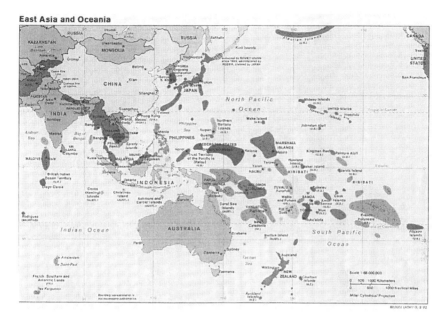

Map of trade areas East of Africa in Oceania

https://legacy.lib.utexas.edu/maps/asia.html

The return trip from the EU should prove to be just as profitable and as safe as the trip going there in the first place. They can trade in Djibouti, Sri Lanka, Singapore, Viet Nam or even one of the Chinese cities back on the way to Tianjin. Even Taiwan may become a trading partner. Storage for these valuable goods; Chinese sneakers and clothes, Arab oil, German Cars and other commodities picked up on the routes will be a matter of convenience and cost.

Some ships will store these goods at the cheapest places possible; most likely Viet Nam and Hainan. Others will store them in cities on the way or back from Tianjin, the shipping city of Beijing. Beijing does not have a harbor, and will be highly dependent on Tianjin. There will be ample storage areas in Tianjin, Shanghai, Ningbo, Fuzhou, Xiamen and Quanzhou, as well as Guangzhou and Shenzhen. Hainan and Macao could also be ample storage areas. Hong Kong would not be advisable as a storage area because space there is extremely expensive for both ships and cargo.

The Southern Overland Route

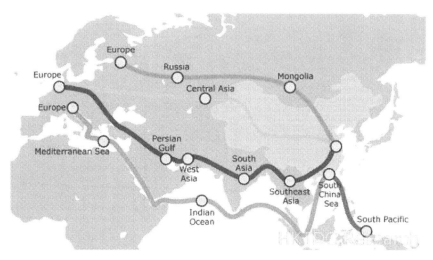

Map of the Proposed Southern Overland Route

https://www.2wglobal.com/news-and-insights/articles/features/
one-belt-one-road-the-future-for-trade-between-east-and-west/

This map gives a very good idea of the Southern Overland Route in orange. However, the connections of Xian and Beijing may or may not be practical. The connection from Urumqi to Kazakhstan, Uzbekistan, Turkmenistan, and Iran to Turkey, and then possibly on to Russia, is far more probable.

In addition to geographical problems for the Southern Overland Route, there are socio-economic problems as well. These lie within the Muslim community of Urumqi, which has been a problem for the CPC in the past. Currently, the CPC has several detention centers for discontented Muslim-Chinese near and around Urumqi. This was in response to the brutal slaying of Han Chinese by mobs of Muslim Chinese in recent race riots in Urumqi. It was one of the very few places in China where there were race riots; far fewer than in the United States, for example.

In retaliation, Han Chinese killed several Muslim Chinese, and the situation become extremely polarized. Now the Chinese government has set up these camps for Muslim Chinese in the area for two reasons: to protect Han Chinese from further violence, and to protect the Muslim Chinese from violence from the Han Community. The Belt and Road Initiative may provide a solution to several of these problems.

One major cause of unrest from the Muslim community is a lack of good jobs. The Muslim community contends that almost all the good jobs go to Han Chinese, and there is some documentation to show this may be the case. But if the Southern Overland Route develops to its second stage (infrastructure development before implementation), then it will be primarily Muslim Chinese from the Urumqi area that will be filling most of the jobs. Why? Because the countries slated for the Southern Overland Route to pass through to Turkey are all predominantly Muslim.

Han Chinese are nowhere nearly as comfortable about working in primarily Muslim countries as Muslim Chinese. In addition to cultural similarities, another benefit will be to provide jobs for a Chinese minority that is currently repressed in Urumqi. Economic parity will go a long way to solving the differences between the two groups. The camps may eventually be discontinued if the Southern Overland Route infrastructure plans proceed without incident. The Muslim community within Urumqi will then begin to achieve economic parity with the Han Chinese community of the city as well.

Infrastructure projects have already begun in Kazakhstan, a country nearby Urumqi. More are planned for Uzbekistan and Turkmenistan. Eventually, Iran and Turkey will need major projects as well. The Muslim Chinese population will come in very handy for these proposed projects as well. It appears to be a win-win situation for the CPC and China.

After Completion

After completion of the infrastructure of this route, some difficult decisions will lie ahead for China. The route ends in Turkey. It will be Turkey and China that make the ultimate decisions as to where Chinese goods will be shipped; most likely to Eastern Europe or Southern Russia. A third alternative will be shipping goods to the

Mideast through Iran. All of these schemes will most likely involve Chinese sneakers and clothes as its primary export. The moderate quality and low price of manufactured Chinese goods will be very attractive to all three areas mentioned above.

In essence, China will become the Walmart of the Belt and Road; with moderate quality at a very low price, the Walmart formula. This will make billions of dollars in profit for China in these regions and eat into the Western, and particularly, the American market shares, for these products. Some Western companies, who already have mass production in China, will benefit, but several others will not, as Chinese companies with their own lines of sneakers and clothes will easily be able to undercut them.

Getting back to the three final destinations of Chinese goods, China is faced with a few problems. Russia must be included in both this scheme and the Maritime route in order for China to sell oil obtained from Saudi Arabia to any countries on either of the Belt and Road routes. Russia will be very protective of its market share for oil in both the EU and in Eastern Europe. Germany may be off the table for China for oil trade. China might find little competition in Central Asia and Africa, as well as Asia and Oceania. This will probably be their primary market for Saudi Arabian oil.

Map of the Northern Route in Orange

http://bruce-humes.com/archives/9692

The Northern Overland Route

Preliminary Plans for the Northern Overland Route

Our substantial army of researchers show The Northern Overland Route is the third and most difficult plan for the Belt and Road Initiative. Originating in either Beijing or Urumqi, and possibly passing through Xian, this plan has a few severe problems. First, and foremost, is the weather. The weather in Mongolia and Siberia is horrendous during the Winter. Protecting sensitive high-speed rail equipment in this type of weather will be a major challenge for China. Temperatures of 60 degrees below Fahrenheit are not uncommon here. Safety will be a major concern. This problem may be resolved by shifting the point of origin from Siberia to Mongolia.

But the primary concern for Beijing and the CPC for this route will be control. Who will control the goods on these trains? After the trains leave Chinese territory, Russia will be in primary control of both the trains and the goods. After the goods arrive in Moscow, Russia will determine whether they go to EU, Eastern Europe, Scandinavia, or stays in Russia. China will have its preferences as well, but their preferences will take second place to the preferences of Russia.

China may not care too much where Russia sends the goods, as long as the goods are sold. But this lack of control might pose a problem for them. As a great Chinese leader once said "it doesn't matter if the cat is black or white, as long as it catches the mouse" (Deng Xiaoping).

Chapter Two

---⁂---

Hong Kong Alternatives - Reducing Docking and Storage Fees

Map of Hainan

https://www.chinadiscovery.com/sanya-tours/maps.html

The most logical departure point in China for the planned Maritime Route to the untrained eye would be Hong Kong. But Hong Kong is the most expensive city in China to do business in several areas. Renting office space, docking spaces, and storage units in Hong Kong would be more expensive than every other city in coastal China. It would be like renting office space, docking space or storage space in Manhattan, New York.

The CPC and Xi Jinping have taken prudent steps to reduce these financial burdens on both SOEs and private Chinese businesses. Xi has recently just closed a multi-billion dollar deal with Hainan to augment Hong Kong as a departure site for the Maritime Belt and Road Initiative. This will provide a much less expensive alternative to Hong Kong. It will still behoove SOEs and private Chinese companies to have offices and operate out of Hong Kong; that is why the mainland connected its high-speed rail to the city. They also have the cooperation of Hong Kong Mayor Lam for several other projects.

But several private companies will be looking for absolutely the lowest operating expenses for their companies. This is where Hainan and several other options for the origin point of the Maritime Belt and Road will take place. Other options will include: Tianjin, Shanghai, Ningbo, Fuzhou, Xiamen, Quanzhou, Shenzhen, Guangzhou, and Macau, among others. Let us examine each alternative for benefits and drawbacks.

Hainan

Hainan would become the South-Westernmost point in China, making it the perfect departure point from mainland China to begin the Maritime Belt and Road. The cost of its docking fees, rental space (away from the tourist areas), and cost of storage units will be far lower than those within Hong Kong. The area is also closer to the first stop of the Maritime Belt and Road area, Viet Nam. There is one additional advantage to this location; it is convenient to Kunming, a major Chinese city in the Southwestern part of China which will want to cash in on the Belt and Road as well.

Hainan appears to be the perfect solution to China for the Maritime Belt and Road departure point from the mainland. But looks can be deceiving. Hainan is also the most remote area in China from all the other major cities of Northeastern, Central, Northern, and Eastern China. It is only convenient to the Southwest of China. This would be great for Hong Kong itself (other than losing some business), Macao, Shenzhen, Guangzhou, Kunming, Quanzhou, and Xiamen. But cities in all other places will have logistical problems reaching Hainan.

So, in retrospect, cities not included in the short list mentioned above, will have to look for alternatives to Hainan. This translates into shipping by high-speed rail or by truck, to precisely the cities that are in relative proximity to Hainan. So the list mentioned above will also be a list for prospective alternatives to Hainan as well.

Map of Macao

https://www.chinadiscovery.com/assets/images/hongkong/
maps/hong-kong-china-map-full.jpg

Macau

There is a joke circulating in Beijing that Chinese businessmen doing business in Macau for the Belt and Road will have to have a line in their budgets for gambling. Chinese businessmen have a reputation for being high rollers, and there is no better (or worse, depending on you perspective) place to do business for high rollers than Macau. And contrary to rumor, these businessmen will not lose half their cargoes of their shipments gambling at Macau casinos.

Macau is ideally situated close to the Chinese mainland, close to Hong Kong and close to Hainan as well. It is fairly remote from the Northwest, Central China, Northern China, and Eastern China. These are the same drawbacks that Hainan and Hong Kong have for these cities. The Tianjin solution, which we will discuss later, might be the best solution for these remote Chinese areas.

Macau will have much cheaper docking facilities than Hong Kong, but not as cheap as Hainan. They will also offer cheaper rental spaces for offices and storage than Hong Kong. But once again, these rental spaces for offices and storage will not be as inexpensive as Hainan as property values (outside of the tourist areas of Hainan) in Macau are higher than Hainan.

Without a doubt, the gambling casinos will be a major attraction for Chinese mainland businessmen operating ships on the Maritime Route. Hopefully, they will not lose any of those ships while gambling there.

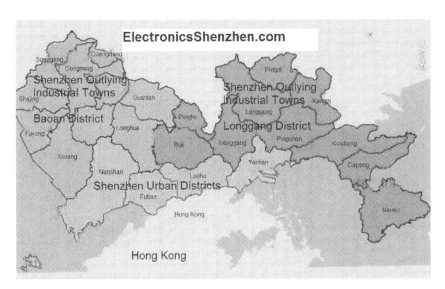

Map of Shenzhen

http://www.electronicsshenzhen.com/wp-content/gallery/
maps/Shenzhen%20Town%20Borders4.jpg

Shenzhen

Shenzhen will be a major consideration for Chinese businessmen to be a departure point for the Maritime Route as well. It is located directly Northeast of Macau. It is also conveniently located in close proximity to Southwestern Chinese cities and ports, it will have relatively lower docking, rental spaces for offices and storage, but most importantly, it is in close proximity to several of the primary goods that will be produced and shipped on the Maritime Belt and Road.

These would be Shenzhen sneakers and clothes. Along with Guangzhou, a city very close by, the extra benefit of having goods you will be shipping on the Maritime Route right next to your office space, storage space, and docking facilities could be an unbeatable combination for several Chinese companies. The only drawback, which may be a minor consideration for several companies, is that the location of Shenzhen is far away from Central China, Northern China, and Eastern China. For companies with factories in Shenzhen, however, there will be very few options that offer more advantages than Shenzhen.

Map of Guangzhou

http://www.beijingholiday.com/guangzhou-tours/guangzhou-maps.html

Guangzhou

Guangzhou offers almost all the same advantages that Shenzhen offers, at a fraction of the price of doing business in Hong Kong. There are several sneaker and clothes factories conveniently located next to Guangzhou's waterways and for companies selling to Oceania, Africa, the Mideast and Eastern Europe, there are few options better or less expensive than doing business in Guangzhou. Once again, however, the location of Guangzhou is not ideal for businesses in Central China, Northern China, and Eastern China.

Guangzhou is convenient to Hong Kong, so a larger company can have offices in Hong Kong as well as operating offices in Guangzhou. This would be key for companies considering doing business for German cars and Saudi Arabian oil; they will need offices in Hong Kong. Storage of these goods, however, is another thing altogether. Storage in Guangzhou will be far less expensive than storage in Hong Kong.

Map of Quanzhou

http://toursmaps.com/quanzhou-map.html

Quanzhou

This option for the Maritime Belt and Road Route is interesting from a Centralist perspective. Quanzhou is approximately equidistant from both Eastern and Southwestern China. It could possibly be a perfect midpoint storage or docking area for businesses doing operations from Beijing, Tianjin, Shanghai, Ningbo, or Fuzhou. The only competition for Quanzhou for this type of situation would be Xiamen, which has a very similar location and two additional advantages; their proximity to Taiwan and their proximity to Hong Kong.

Quanzhou will be cheaper than Hong Kong, Hainan, Macau, Shenzhen or Guangdong, but not by a prohibitive amount of money. Quanzhou has almost as good as access to Taiwan as Xiamen does, if a company plans to do business with Taiwan within the Belt and Road. Of course, they may run into strict CPC guidelines for doing business with Taiwan; but most companies will be able to get it done.

Map of Xiamen

http://travelsfinders.co/xiamen-map-2.html

Xiamen

Xiamen is also part of the Centralist perspective. It too, is approximately the same distance from both Eastern and Southwestern

China. Like Quanzhou, it could be a perfect selection for businesses already located in Xiamen and surrounding areas. It would make a very cost effective midpoint docking area for places like Beijing, Tianjin, Shanghai or Ningbo. Storage space in Xiamen would quite inexpensive as well, when compared to other Chinese port cities.

The big aces in the hole for Xiamen is Taiwan, which is very close to Xiamen and the fact that it is closer to Hong Kong than Quanzhou. The potential for massive electronic trade between Taiwan and Xiamen could make Xiamen a big player in the Maritime Belt and Road scheme. One additional asset for Xiamen is Jimei University in the northern part of Xiamen. They train thousands of Chinese navel cadets every year for the Chinese Navy, who will be an integral part of the Maritime Route strategies.

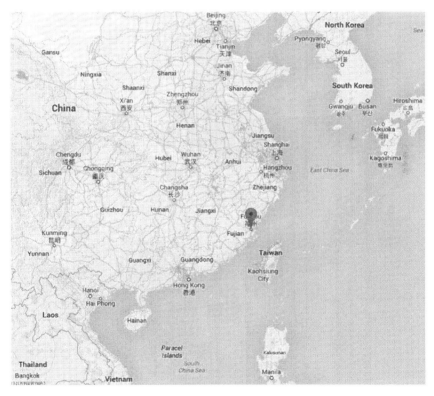

Map of Fuzhou

https://www.travelchinaguide.com/cityguides/
fujian/fuzhou/subway-metro-map.htm

Fuzhou

Fuzhou is the provincial capital of Fujian; the province where Quanzhou, Xiamen and Fuzhou are all located. Fuzhou has great proximity to Taipei, the capital of Taiwan. It should be interesting to watch the power struggle among the three cities for the biggest pieces of the pie for the Maritime Route; especially for docking, storage and business offices. Fuzhou, as the capital of the province, would have to be considered the favorite to get these prize concessions, but businesses will make up their own minds which area offers the best business conditions.

One advantage of Fuzhou is that it is closer to Ningbo, Shanghai, Tianjin and Beijing and its southern neighboring cities. Of course, an advantage going to the Maritime Route is a disadvantage coming back from the Maritime Route. Ideally, a city that is halfway between the other Chinese ports is immune to the problem of being equidistant from or too close to the Northern cities or Southwestern cities. Quanzhou and Xiamen are the only two Chinese cities that clearly fall into the Centralist Strategy.

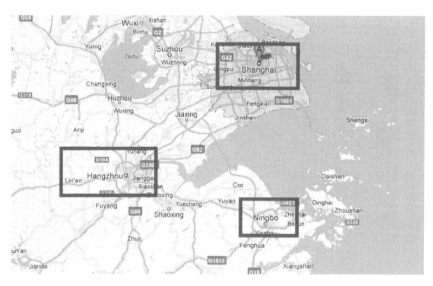

Map of Ningbo

https://cdn5.loyaltylobby.com/wp-content/gallery/september-2012/
xpark-hyatt-ningbo-shanghai-map.jpg.pagespeed.ic.7CdYQ1Hj_h.jpg

Ningbo

Ningbo does not have an ideal location for the Maritime Belt and Road; nor does it have an ideal location for the Southern Overland Route. So Ningbo will have to do some creative marketing and planning in order to benefit from the Belt and Road Initiative. The only advantage that Ningbo has in this scheme is that its office space, docking fees and storage fees will be cheaper than Shanghai, its neighbor across the river. But Ningbo has a serious recognition factor; people recognize the name of Shanghai to a far greater degree than Ningbo. Shanghai also has a much greater international history than Ningbo.

Ningbo is closer to ships coming back from the Maritime Route than Shanghai, and, conversely, it is further away for ships leaving from Tianjin. But if the ships are leaving and returning to various ports like Shanghai, Ningbo or Tianjin, it really does not make much of a difference in nautical miles. All things considered, Ningbo is a good selection for lower costs.

Map of Shanghai

https://www.yangtze-river-cruises.com/shanghai-tours/shanghai-maps.html

Shanghai

Shanghai has traditionally been the financial nerve center of mainland China. Recently, Beijing has tried, but failed, to take the place of Shanghai economically. Beijing simply cannot match the international experience that Shanghai has accumulated over the years.

Shanghai, unfortunately, is located out of the loop for the Southern Overland Route of the Belt and Road, and is very far East of the Maritime Route as well. One plan that might work for Shanghai is to have ships originate from the city, and stop at Sri Lanka or Djibouti on the way up to the Red Sea.

The ships would have the option of taking inexpensive Chinese goods such as sneakers and clothes and to sell them to India via Sri Lanka, or to Egypt via the Red Sea. They could also continue on to Turkey and sell their goods to Southern Russia or to Eastern Europe. If they wanted to take a riskier venture, they could buy oil from Saudi Arabia and then sell it to either Eastern Europe or Germany. This last option would make a lot of money for Shanghai, but it might cause political problems with Russia, the economic competitor of Saudi Arabia for the oil market in the EU and Eastern Europe.

Beijing and the CPC might prohibit Shanghai ships from engaging in the oil trade, if it might endanger the entire Belt and Road project. Shanghai would then have to bring the entire load of oil back to Oceania and India, where there would be no objection by Russia to sell oil to neighbors close to China. Both the Maritime Route and the Southern Overland Route will be prohibited from selling oil to Russian clients in most cases.

Map of Tianjin

Tianjin

Tianjin is a key component in the Maritime Route for only one reason; it is the lifeline to the sea for Beijing. Without Tianjin, Beijing has no access to the sea, so they will include Tianjin in every aspect of the Maritime Route. Unfortunately for Tianjin, this same process does not hold true for either the Southern or Northern Overland routes; which Beijing will handle completely by themselves. However, Tianjin can still make some nice profits, gain access to oil and German luxury cars and other benefits by being the conduit for Beijing on the Maritime Belt and Road.

Ships will be inexpensively moored in Tianjin and will leave primarily with one of two cargoes: either they will leave with nothing at all in their holds, and load up with Saudi Arabian oil, or they will load up with Chinese sneakers and clothes, as well as a few other low-end Chinese commodities. Tianjin ships leaving the city empty will most likely be headed to Saudi Arabia and back, unless they have permission to sell oil to the EU and Easte. rn Europe. This will be difficult to do because of Russia. However, if Russia permits limited trades to Germany in exchange for luxury German cars, China can pledge they will not sell oil to Eastern Europe, and Russia will be able to keep its monopolies alive there.

Cargoes carrying inexpensive Chinese commodities will be welcome in a slew of countries; all the way from China to Vietnam, to Singapore, to Sri Lanka, to Djibouti, to Saudi Arabia, to Egypt, to Turkey, to Greece, to Italy and to Germany or Russia, as well as Eastern Europe and the rest of the EU, Oceania, and Africa. On the return trip, the Tianjin ships will peel off a few hundred barrels of oil, a few dozen luxury cars and a bit of cash for their time and trouble. Everyone will partake in the profits. It is only a half hour by bullet train to Beijing from Tianjin.

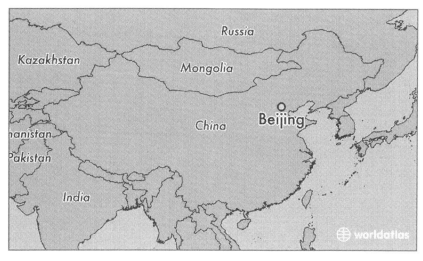

Map of Beijing

https://www.worldatlas.com/img/locator/city/075/3575-beijing-locator-map.jpg

Beijing

Beijing is the queen of the prom; the king of the mountain, the big boss. It will tell every other city in China where to go, how much to trade, what they can trade, how they can trade, and who they can trade to. They will be in all three of the Belt and Road plans; not just as a participant, but as a full-time supervisor of all three. The CPC in Beijing will be running the entire show from start to finish for all three routes. The only exception might be the third Northern Overland Route, which will be travelling primarily through Russia. Russia will most likely be running the show for that route; especially after the goods reach Moscow, where China has little, if any, control.

Beijing is a landlocked city; it will be highly dependent on Tianjin for access to the Maritime Route. It will only take one half hour to ship goods from Beijing to Tianjin by bullet train. Ships docked in Tianjin will be awaiting orders from Beijing on what cargo, if any, they will be carrying, and precisely what route that will be taking on the Maritime Road. Cargoes to and from Beijing will vary widely, as will stopping points along the way of the Maritime Route. Beijing will have to share (in small proportions) some of their cargoes and profits with Tianjin.

Items exported from Beijing via Tianjin will include Chinese sneakers and clothes, Chinese herbal medicines, and other Chinese commodities. Primary Beijing imports will be Saudi Arabian oil, German luxury cars, and various tech and electronic components. Heavy machinery for infrastructure work may either be imported or exported, depending on the complexity of the machines.

China and Beijing will have to have measured responses to Russian irritation over oil purchases and distribution from Saudi Arabia. Interfering or competing with Russian oil markets in the EU would probably be ill-advised for Beijing. Beijing might have a smoother road with oil imports and distribution if they sell their Saudi Arabian oil to Oceania, Southeast Asia, Africa and other areas rather than to the EU. Alienating Russia would be a very bad idea for the Chinese Belt and Road Initiative plans.

Importing luxury German cars, or even low end German cars such as Volkswagen will require a bit of planning and maneuvering by Beijing. Sending oil directly to Germany for German luxury cars would be the easiest, but most dangerous process. The process would be simple enough: stop at a northern Italian port, drop off the Saudi Arabian oil, and then have it sent directly to Germany. Germany, then, would have no problem sending back their cars via Italian bullet trains to the Italian ports.

There is only one problem with this scenario; China and Beijing would be tampering with the Russian market share of oil sold in the EU. This would most likely be unacceptable to Russia, and severely affect other Belt and Road markets within Eastern European and the EU. China and Beijing are too smart to allow this problem to develop. They will come up with alternatives for purchasing and distributing oi from Saudi Arabia, and for purchasing luxury cars from Germany.

One possible solution will be to sell the Arabian oil to African countries, Asian countries and all the areas along the Maritime Belt and Road after entering the Suez Canal returning to China. They can still pick up luxury German cars at northern Italian ports, but they will be paying electronically for them with profits derived from their oil sales to the above areas rather than Eastern Europe or the EU. This will actually speed up the process because Chinese ships will not have to load any oil on the bullet trains going to Germany; they will just have to wait for the German shipments of cars and then merely sail away.

Chapter Three

The Problem of Inclusion - Strategies for Including as many Chinese cities as possible in the Belt and Road Initiative

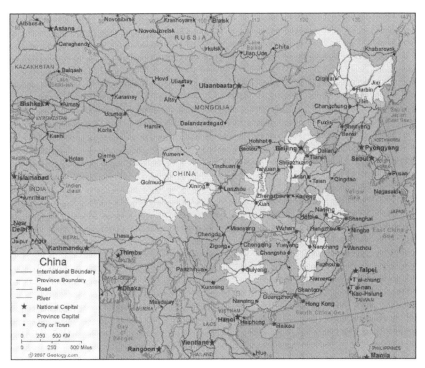

Major Chinese Cities

https://www.china-mike.com/china-travel-tips/
tourist-maps/major-chinese-cities-map/

Inclusion of All Chinese Cities

Every city in China will want to be part of the Belt and Road Initiative. CPC officials in Beijing will have to carefully plan inclusion for every city in China to be involved in at least one aspect or route of the Belt and Road Initiative. This will not be a simple task for either Beijing or for many of the cities that want to be included. Ultimately, it will be the proactive efforts of each city that will determine the level of their participation. Most cities will not be handed participation on a silver platter; they will have to fight for their own city's market share and participation in the process. Let's take a look at the map of China and tick off the major cities that will almost certainly be involved:

Let us begin with the Northeastern cities. We have included just about every important Northeastern Chinese city, and possibly a few that are not that important. But better to err on the side of excess, rather than deletion. We have already discussed the strategies of Beijing in detail, so we will skip them; they will be in charge of all three main Belt and Road Initiative routes. We can make small groupings where cities have very little differences in distance and import/export commodities.

As of 2019, Northeastern China has been replaced by Beijing as the starting point of the Northern Overland Route with a stop in Mongolia toward the West, rather than going East via Siberia.

Hohhot

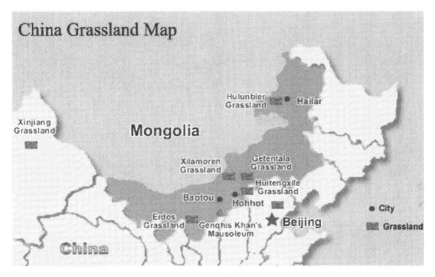

Map of Hohhot

https://www.chinadiscovery.com/inner-mongolia/hohhot.html

Hohhot is directly Northwest of Beijing, and really not too far from that important Chinese city. This city could be the first stop for the Northern Overland Route if the Mongolian route is eventually chosen over the Siberian route; a good choice for weather purposes.

Hohhot produces prime lamb for several cities in China, and would now be able to ship its lamb West to other destinations. The Belt and Road is absolutely essential to the success of the Mongolian economy.

Map of Talyuan

https://www.chinadiscovery.com/taiyuan-tours/maps.html

Taiyuan is Southwest of Beijing and directly South of Hohhot, the much more likely first stop on the Northern Overland Route. Taiyuan will not have much economic leverage in this Belt and Road route, but will have two options. They can ship to Beijing by truck or train and then onward West to Hohhot, or they can truck or train to Hohhot directly, although this may not necessarily be the most efficient plan. Time and cost will eventually dictate the decisions by Taiyuan.

Map of Badaling

http://beijingservice.com/greatwall/badalinggreatwalltour.htm

Badaling

There is pretty much nothing of economic value in Badaling outside of the tremendous tourism attraction of the Great Wall. For that reason alone, Beijing may opt to include Badaling in the Northern Overland Route as a tourist attraction for trading partners. Even though Badaling is North of Beijing and not directly on the path to Hohhot, it may be included with a quick bullet train line; something well within the capabilities of China to accomplish quickly.

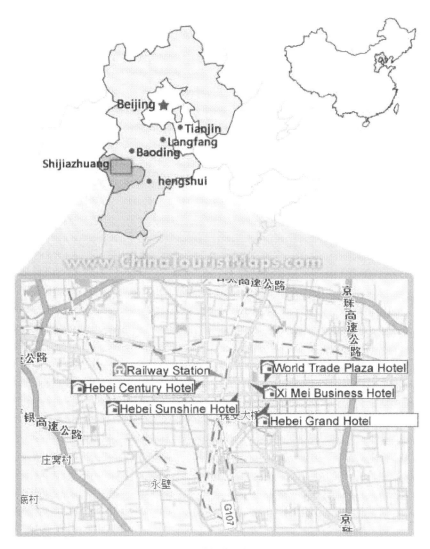

Map of Shijiazhuang

http://www.chinatouristmaps.com/hotel/shijiazhuang.html

Shijiazhuang

As one can see from the map above, Shijiazhuang is just a bit Southwest of Beijing and relatively close to the other connecting cities that may be involved indirectly in the Northern Overland Route. This city will have to truck or train to Beijing or to Hohhot, depending on the time and money involved in any shipping scheme.

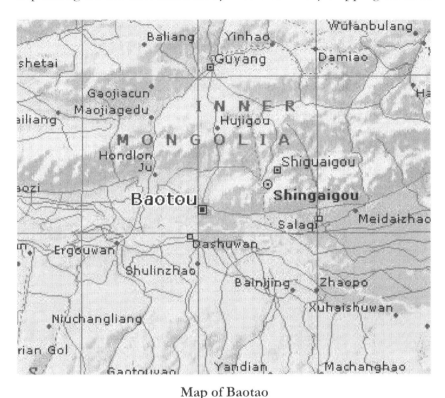

Map of Baotao

http://www.china-tour.cn/Baotou/

Baotau is directly West of Beijing and most likely will not be included in the main Northern Overland Route. However, Baotau does have one option; it can truck or train to Hohhot directly as a secondary source of materials not available in Beijing. It will most decidedly play a minor role in the route, however.

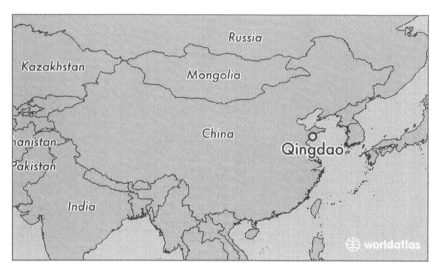

Map of Qingdao

https://www.worldatlas.com/img/locator/city/068/3268-qingdao-locator-map.jpg

Qingdao

As we can see from the map above, Qingtao is not really in a very good place for the Northern Overland Route. It is almost equidistant from Beijing and Shanghai, so it has no special location advantage. However, it does have three options for trucking and train shipments; it can ship to Beijing, Tianjin or Shanghai, depending on which route they intend to use.

They will be the most distant route outside of Beijing for the Maritime Route, but that problem might be mitigated by shipping to Tianjin. If they opt for the Northern Overland Route, they will be roughly in the same shipping boat as Xian, which is also far from the planned routes. Qingtao will most likely be a secondary Chinese city in any of the routes.

Map of Dalian

https://internchina.com/wp-content/uploads/
Photo-3-Internchina-Dalian-on-map.gif

Dalian

Dalian is a port city in Northeastern China, and the gateway to Siberia in the Northeast corridor of trade. There is also a thriving trade with both Koreas in Dalian harbor. These Korean contacts may provide goods that might be used in Northern Overland Route shipments to Hohhot. Considering the geographical location of Dalian, they would most likely be left out of the Maritime Route.

Hohhot, Tianjin, Beijing, Taiyuan, Badaling, Shijiazhuang, Baotou, Qingdao, and Dalian

These Northeastern cities have more options than their neighbors to the Northeast. They may not be able to trade with Russia as easily, but they will have shipping access via Tianjin to the Maritime Route. In addition, they will be geographically closer than their Northeastern neighbors to the Southern Overland Route. Their proximity to Urumqi will be an asset. If the Southern Overland route initiates from Beijing, it will be an added bonus to all of these cities.

41

But even if this route begins in Urumqi instead of Beijing, they will have greater access than cities either above or below them in China.

Politically and economically, it might be wiser for these cities to tie their wagon to Beijing rather than cities outside of Beijing's direct influence. Beijing is still the prime mover for all three routes, and will determine which cities will benefit the most from their strategies.

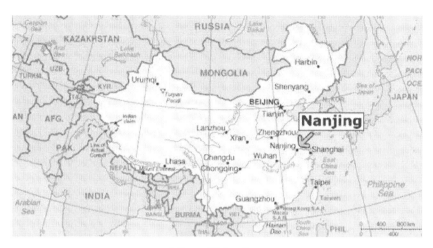

Map of Nanjing

https://www.yangtze-river-cruises.com/assets/images/
destinations/nanjing/maps/nanjing-china-map-500.jpg

Nanjing

Nanjing is much closer to Shanghai than Beijing or Tianjin. This would be a very good indication that its primary strategy would be to tie itself with Shanghai for the Maritime Route. Shipping directly to Shanghai would most likely be the only financially viable option for Nanjing. Prospects for inclusion will most likely be of a secondary nature.

Map of Shanghai

https://www.yangtze-river-cruises.com/shanghai-tours/shanghai-maps.html

Shanghai

One way or the other, you can bank on Shanghai being included as an essential player for either the Northern Overland Route from Beijing, or the Maritime Route to Southern China. It may even find its way into the Southern Overland Route through Urumqi with direct bullet train shipments to that city. Shanghai is the most economically advanced city in mainland China, although not on par with Hong Kong yet. Some might disagree with that assessment, but Hong Kong has a far more favorable location. Beijing and Shanghai have a quiet, but ferocious, competition for Chinese business on the mainland.

Beijing, however, will be calling the political shots, so the current money is still on Beijing. Shanghai will gets its piece of the pie, though.

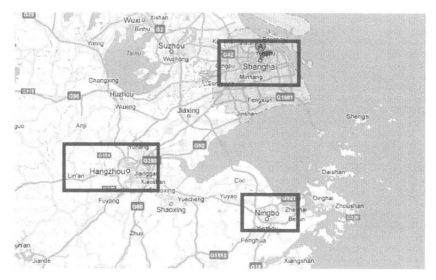

Map of Ningbo

https://loyaltylobby.com/2012/10/01/park-hyatt-ningbo/

Ningbo is a large urban area directly south of Shanghai. Costs for living in Ningbo are considerably less than those living in Shanghai, but the large body of water separating the two cities makes for a very inconvenient obstacle. A train to Hangzhou and then on to Shanghai is your fastest option, but it is still inconvenient. Despite this inconvenience, several thousand commuters make this trip daily.

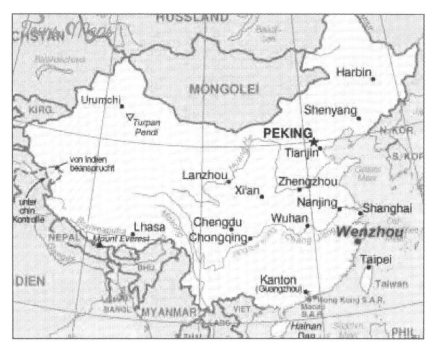

Map of Wenzhou

http://toursmaps.com/wenzhou-map.html

Wenzhou is closer to Southern China than it is to Beijing. It is relatively close to Shanghai as well, and not too far away from Taiwan. Wenzhou is a prosperous, dirty city with foul air caused by pollution trapped within a valley area surrounded by mountains; quite similar to Los Angeles. Despite the pollution, the area is very modern, has good Western food, and several thousand prosperous professionals.

Map of Shantou

https://www.weather-forecast.com/locations/Shantou/forecasts/latest

This map of Shantou highlights its economic potential due to its close proximity to the points of origin for the Maritime Route of the Belt and Road. There are several investment opportunities for this city because of its location and relatively low rental costs for both private and business residences. It is closer to Hong Kong than Xiamen, Quanzhou, or Fuzhou.

Nanjing, Shanghai, Ningbo, Wenzhou, and Shantou

The city ports on the East Coast of China have a great number of similarities, but each has a unique advantage as well. Nanjing is closer to inland China, and therefore a good candidate to be included in any Northern or Southern Overland route. Shanghai has a great European guanxi or networking history, Ningbo is south of Shanghai, and is closer to Hong Kong, Fuzhou is the capital of Fujian, and so dictates policy for its competition in Xiamen and Quanzhou. Xiamen, however is closest to Taiwan. And Quanzhou is close to Taiwan as well. Shantou is the closest of all to Hong Kong, and is a great choice for storage or docking facilities at a much lower price than Hong Kong.

None of these cities has unique export items, with the possible exception of Shanghai, which can import foreign experts from Europe and the US to several points along the Belt and Road Routes. Inclusion of other routes would be minimal for Shanghai; they will most likely live or die with the Maritime Route for investment opportunities.

Central China: Ningxia, Lanzhou, Zhengzhou, Xian, Kaifeng, Xinning, Wuhan, Chengdu, Mianyang. Guiyang, and Nanning

Location of Ningxia

https://ningxiaunveiled.wordpress.com/

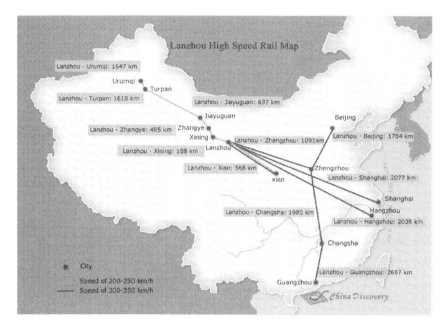

Map of Lanzhou

https://www.chinadiscovery.com/assets/images/china-train-
tour/maps/lanzhou-high-speed-rail-map.jpg

Lanzhou

Lanzhou is centrally located in China. This is both a good and
bad situation. It is good because it has access to the East Coast and to
The Southern Overland Route starting in Urumqi. It is bad because it
is still a pretty good distance from both. This is a case of the glass
being half-filled or half-empty.

Location of Xian

https://upload.wikimedia.org/wikipedia/commons/a/a7/Xi%27an_location.png

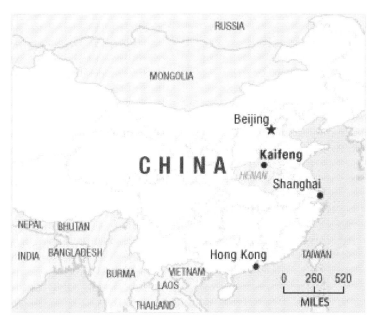

Map of Kaifeng

https://www.npr.org

Map of Xining

http://www.chinagreattravel.com/images/maps/city/xining.jpg

Location of Wuhan

https://www.chinadiscovery.com/assets/images/
wuhan/maps/wuhan-china-map-full.jpg

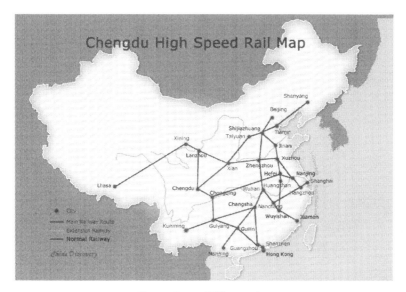

Location of Chengdu

https://www.chinadiscovery.com/assets/images/Train/maps/

chengdu-rail-map/chengdu-high-speed-railway-map-866.jpg

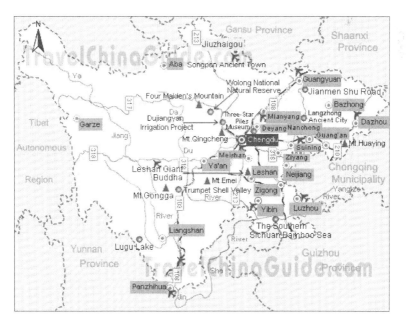

Map of Mianyang

http://travelsfinders.com/mianyang-map-tourist-attractions.html

Map of Guiyang

https://www.chinadiscovery.com/guiyang-tours/maps.html

Location of Nanning

http://www.chinatouradvisors.com/travelguide/Nanning/

Cities included in Central China that will have to compete for market share in the Belt and Road Initiative are numerous. Most of these cities will be in the same situation, and have little to differentiate themselves from their competition. But there are a few exceptions. Xian has the Terra Cotta Warriors and more tourism than most other cities. So this will give them an opportunity to take advantage of the Belt and Road with some careful investments.

Kaifeng has a long and storied history as being a shelter for Westerners besieged in Europe, including a very long history of sheltering migrating Jews. It has the largest Jewish population in China, and a great deal of literary tradition as well, as several Jewish writers were accomplished authors who wrote while in China. These contacts could eventually prove to be useful for future Belt and Road considerations. Chengdu is noted for Chinese milk, and may be a strong exporter of such. All of the other cities must create a new personality to attract international business. Right now, they are just well-known in China.

Of all these cities, Nanning is the best-positioned location-wise. It is in very close proximity to Hong Kong, and has much lower costs for rents for both private and business residences.

Western China: Urumqi, Kunming, Lhasa

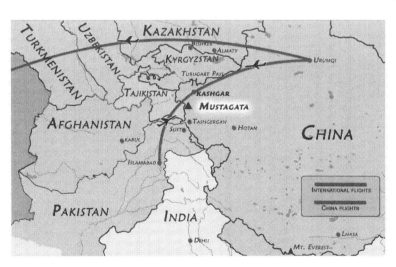

Location of Urumqi

https://www.chinadiscovery.com/urumqi-tours/maps.html

Map of Kunming

http://www.klia2.info/images/airasia/china-map-en.jpg

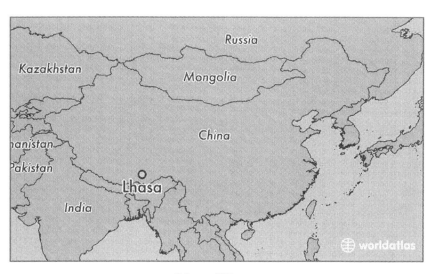

Map of Lhasa

https://www.worldatlas.com/as/cn/54/where-is-lhasa.html

The Western cities of China have their own unique opportunities and problems. Urumqi seems to be the most promising Western Chinese city of them all. They are ideally located on the cusp of the Southern Overland Route that leaves China and enters Kazakhstan. This will provide wonderful employment opportunities for a city that is in current chaos due to internal racial and religious strife. Urumqi Muslims are in a current feud with Han Chinese within the city. It has even escalated into roaming gangs that killed and injured large numbers of the opposition. It has also led to the creation of detention centers in the province occupied by Urumqi.

The majority of people being held in these detention centers are Muslim Chinese. The government is Han Chinese. The Southern Overland Route may be the last good chance for both factions to come out of this conflict in decent economic shape. The Chinese government would love for the Muslim Chinese in Urumqi and surrounding areas to work in the primarily Muslim countries they are building up for the Southern Overland Route.

The Muslim community in these areas would love to have these jobs as well. Improved economic conditions among Muslim Chinese would virtually eradicate the racial tensions between Muslim and Han Chinese. And China would be able to have a Chinese presence in the workforce outside of China and inside these Muslim countries. A win-win for everyone. The city of Urumqi could grow a great deal, and it could become the hub of Western and Northern China.

The prospects are not quite as bright for Lhasa, which is a Buddhist stronghold. However, they could become involved in the Maritime Route somehow, and help with infrastructure in Southeast Asia, another Buddhist stronghold. The same principle that might work for Urumqi could possibly work for Lhasa as well, but the path will be more difficult for them. Other cities in Western China are pretty much out of the picture, with the exception of Kunming, which does have a few options.

They can go north to Urumqi, or south to Hainan or Hong Kong. But if they go south, they will have to contend with Viet Nam. Going north is difficult as well, as it is over 500 miles further away than Southeast Asia. Kunming has some complex decisions to make; they probably cannot afford the investments in both of these routes. They will have to pick one or the other, and then put all of their resources into developing the route they eventually pick. There will be little turning back once they make their decision. The Hong Kong route appears to be the favorite at this point.

The Northern Overland Route - Russian vs Chinese Strategies

There are four major areas of concern geographically speaking, for the Northern Overland Route, which is still pretty much in just the planning stages for both Russia and China. This route will have major concerns over weather and control for both countries, as well as final distribution points for Chinese goods arriving at Moscow. The primary areas include Mongolia, Beijing, Siberia, Moscow, and all potential final destinations for this route. Those destinations could include the following: Scandinavia, the EU, or Eastern Europe and Turkey.

We will examine the strategies of all of these areas. As of this writing, the Mongolian option seems to be favored over the Siberian route. This option will garner more control for China, and less control for Russia.

Beijing Route

https://assets.weforum.org/editor/
YcKECzirCXez8ZXbgxKoSPvqwVMH7yYLJ47qFzpFDA0.jpg

We have already examined the concerns and strategies of Beijing for the Maritime Route and its potential as a hub for the Southern Overland Route, but they will most assuredly be the primary origin point of the Northern Overland Route. Both economically and politically, Beijing will look to control every aspect of this route, but will be hard-pressed to match the Russians because of the geographic realities.

Beijing will be exporting the best that China has to offer in exchange for as many German cars as they can purchase from the sales of their exports (and even over and above their sales). Beijing is intent on two things; limiting the influence of Japan on the Chinese economy by importing fewer Japanese cars and more German cars, and two; offsetting the costs of these cars by selling goods to Russia, the EU, Eastern Europe, and Scandinavia.

Beijing is not really interested in Russian oil; they expect to get Saudi Arabian oil at a better price. They may continue to purchase Russian gas, but their oil imports from Russia should go down significantly. Geographically, Beijing will have little control of the trains on this route, once they reach Siberia. However, if the Siberian route is replaced by the Mongolian option, it will change the dynamic of who controls the train cars and content, as well as the final destinations.

Beijing will take special care to not irritate Russia by selling oil to their existing customers in the EU. They will also take care to include Russia in every aspect of the Belt and Road; the Maritime Route through Turkey, the Southern Overland Routh through Turkey, and the Northern Overland Route through either Mongolia, Siberia and Moscow. Hopefully, for China, Russia will not pursue other options for international trade which could harm China. (like a Russia-USA bullet train).

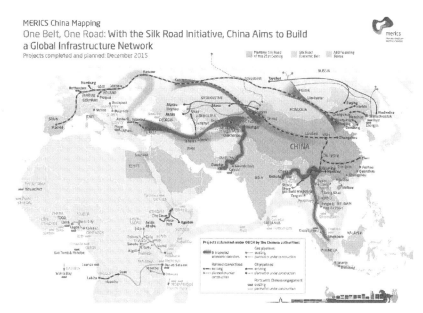

MERICS China Mapping
One Belt, One Road: With the Silk Road Initiative, China Aims to Build
a Global Infrastructure Network
Projects completed and planned: December 2015

Siberian Route

https://www.sott.net

Siberia has two big problems for China within the Northern Belt and Road Initiative for strategies; how will China deal with the weather in Siberia for Chinese bullet trains, and how will China maintain control of products leaving China and entering Siberia and Moscow? These are key questions for China as the costs of the Northern Overland Route will run into the many billions of dollars for them. Let's look at both factors.

First, Siberian winters are legendary. They have among the lowest temperatures and worst snow conditions in the world for any type of transportation. The fact that this route will be well over 2000 miles long with track covered by ice and snow for the vast majority of the distance for several months a year will be an area of great concern for China.

Russian officials will, no doubt, try to soften these details and will try to reassure China that they have all of these things under control. They will mention that they can shield tracks by building elevated platforms in some areas, but the snow comes so fast and heavy, that the weight of the snow may endanger the elevated platform, and cause a severe accident. Also, the several hundreds of miles of unprotected track and track that is not elevated will still pose several dangerous problems.

One problem is how close to the secondary cities should the bullet train come? They cannot run through the center of a city; they are far too fast and dangerous. They will have to be on the outskirts of the cities. If they are on the outskirts of the cities, who will maintain them when bad weather strikes? Very few people live on the outskirts of these minor cities. Some areas have no people at all. How will the track be maintained under these conditions? What about ice? Ice can be even more dangerous than snow.

Part of the deal could be that Russia will maintain the tracks for an extra piece of the pie; not including the Chinese in any of the infrastructure decisions other than the construction of the trains and tracks themselves. Or maybe Russia will build the bullet trains. Then the Chinese participation in the scheme will really become extremely limited and less profitable. In any scenario, there will be several problems for China to overcome this most difficult of all three of the Belt and Road scenarios.

The latest indications are the Siberian route is being tabled in favor of the Mongolian route, which is shorter, faster, and has fewer weather problems. It would take an unanticipated event for China to shift from the Mongolian strategy to the Siberian route.

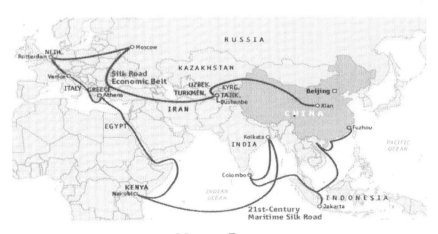

Moscow Route

https://cdn-images-1.medium.com/
max/1600/1*3QLaElAfEuw-Lh9qIofQsQ.jpeg

Moscow will certainly be the prime mover in the Northern Overland Route. As the capital of Russia, it will direct policy all throughout Siberia, within Moscow, and all points to Scandinavia, Eastern Europe, and the EU. It will keep a constant eye on China within the Maritime Route and the Southern Land Route, looking for any incursions into their profitable market shares in oil within the EU, Eastern Europe and Scandinavia. China will have to forego any efforts to make inroads to Russian markets, or face serious economic consequences.

A good strategy for China might be to heavily market Huawei phones, Chinese sneakers and clothes to cities all along Siberia and within Russia, including Moscow, which has thousands of poor people who can use moderate-quality clothing and sneakers at a low price. This Walmart-style marketing strategy has been wildly successful for Walmart in every part of the world. It should be successful using the same formula as Walmart.

Moscow will present another problem for China. They will have almost no control as to where the Chinese goods on this train will go. China will, undoubtedly, want several of these trainloads to go Germany, so they can substantially lessen their balance of payments for German luxury cars; even moderately-priced Volkswagens. But Russia will want to sell these Chinese goods in places that are best for them, not in places that are best for the Chinese.

Russia may want to supply Russia first, then Eastern Europe, then Scandinavia and finally, the EU. However, China after understanding that Russia must be supplied first, will want the next shipment to go to Germany and Italy, while for Russia, it will be more convenient to go to Eastern Europe or Scandinavia. Russia wants to maintain its markets in the EU, and will not allow any variables within their country that will endanger those market shares.

The Mongolian Route

The Mongolian Route will go West from Beijing and avoid taking the perilous Siberian Northern route directly north of Beijing. It will also provide much more Chinese control for Beijing over Moscow, until the train enters Russian territory. Upon entering Russia, most control will be in the hands of the Russians.

Final Destinations for Chinese Goods

Final destinations for Chinese goods for the Northern Overland Route are more problematic for China than both of the other Belt and Road routes. Because Russia will most likely control where the trains stop and go after they leave China, there are several options for the Russians to consider. Russia will most likely schedule these stops for the convenience and profit of Russia, not China. The four primary areas outside of Russia itself will be Turkey, Eastern Europe, Scandinavia, and EU countries.

Scandinavian Route

The Scandinavian Route would include Sweden, Finland, and Norway as well as some surrounding areas. Scandinavia will be keen on receiving low-priced Chinese clothes and shoes of moderate quality. China could become the Walmart of Scandinavia with proper execution of this route's plan.

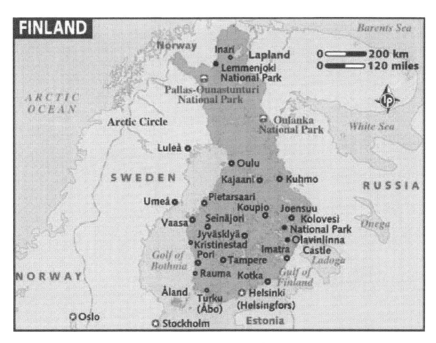

Map of Finland

http://www.rbex.ro/Intermediere-si-consultanta-de-afaceri/Finlanda

Finland

Finland will be the primary entry point for Russia into Scandinavia. From Finland, trains will continue on to both Sweden and Norway. Finland will have a determination on which goods on which trains continue on to other destinations.

Map of Sweden

http://travelsfinders.com/sweden-map.html

Sweden

Sweden should be a major destination within Scandinavia for Russia, China and the Belt and Road. However, there is on small added problem. That problem might be the poor former Soviet Union countries to the south. Shipments to Russia from China could easily be diverted to Estonia, Latvia, Belarus, and Lithuania, among others. There is a larger part of those populations that are poor in relation to the populations within Scandinavia, which are more prosperous.

The former Soviet Union countries might be a better market for inexpensive Chinese clothes and sneakers, rather than Scandinavia. Actual market results will dictate which way this scenario will go.

Map of Norway

http://www.europeword.com/norway.html

Norway

The three countries composing Scandinavia, Norway, Sweden and Finland, will not be major players in any of the Belt and Road schemes. However, they may become minor players in the Northern Overland Route, if Russia so desires. It would be much easier for Russia to route trains from the Northern Overland Route to the EU or Eastern Europe, but if there is money to be made by shipping to Scandinavia, Russia will not leave any money on the table. Be rest assured that Moscow and Siberia, in that order, will take whatever goods it prefers before allowing the rest of any Chinese goods to proceed to Scandinavia or any other destination.

Norway has no particular specialty that either China or Russia desires to the extent either country will go out of its way for Norway. The only scenario that favors Norway is buying Chinese imports of phones, clothes, and sneakers. With the decline of Nokia in China, Scandinavians may be hesitant about buying Huawei phones from China, but they will not hesitate to buy moderate-quality clothes and sneakers at very low prices. The Walmart principle is popular in every country in the world.

Sweden is pretty much in the same boat as Norway, but has a larger population. So Sweden will probably take precedence over Norway, when it comes to goods that might be entering Scandinavia. Moderate-quality clothes and sneakers at very low prices will also be popular in Sweden. Denmark, however, has a bit of edge over its two Scandinavian neighbors.

Norway has a few problems on this route. It is only accessible in the far northern reaches of the country from Russia. The one other possibility is that Russia will build a bullet train route that cuts through the middle of all three Scandinavian countries somewhat to the south of the original entry points. Whether or not that additional infrastructure would be economically rewarding is a matter of conjecture.

Map of Turkey

http://www.optimisetravel.com

Turkey

Turkey is already a major player on the other two routes completely controlled by China. They will not jeopardize the profits that could be made on those two routes by annoying China by trading with Russia on the Northern Overland Route. China wants those goods to go to Eastern Europe or the EU; they really don't want anything that Turkey has to offer. And Turkey already has plenty on its dish from the other two routes. Russia will be well-advised not to ship Chinese goods from Russia to Turkey in this situation. Better for Moscow and Siberia to take what they want first, and then continue on to Eastern Europe or the EU. Both Turkey and Scandinavia look like last resorts for both Russia and China for the Northern Overland Route.

Map of Eastern Europe

https://foreignpolicyblogs.com/2016/11/18/

eastern-europe-duplicitous-tango-moscow-brussels/

Eastern Europe

Eastern Europe will be a primary target for all three of the Belt and Road routes. The Northern Overland Route will be no exception. Why? Because Russia will want to maintain its contacts with countries formally in the USSR, and China will want to exploit one of the best markets in the world for goods of moderate quality offered at a very low price. Eastern Europe needs these Chinese goods; these are not luxury-oriented countries like the EU. The countries in Eastern Europe are just getting by, economically. These goods will be a boost to their economies.

This combination of common Chinese and Russian interests virtually guarantees that the majority of the goods travelling on the Northern Overland Route will be directed toward Eastern European countries; not the EU, Turkey, or Scandinavia. The only possible competition for these goods from this route will come from the EU.

Map of EU Countries

https://www.worldatlas.com/r/w728-h425-c728x425/
upload/2f/fd/ab/regions-of-europe-map.jpg

EU

There are two important questions that must be answered about the EU and the Northern Overland Route: (1) Will the EU get precedence over Eastern Europe for goods shipped by China and Russia on the Northern Overland Route? and (2), if the EU does get precedence; who will be the top-tier EU countries that will be serviced by the Northern Overland Route?

Let's take a look at both of these issues:

1. In our opinion, the EU will not get precedence over Eastern Europe for low-priced Chinese goods travelling

on the Northern Overland Route. Why? Because there are far more poor and working class people in Eastern Europe than there are in EU countries. This bodes well for the demand of inexpensive, moderate quality goods from China. A second reason is that Eastern Europe is closer to Russia than the EU countries. Distance equals additional cost; that, in turn, increases the prices of goods. There is more of a profit-margin selling to Eastern Europe for both China and Russia.

2. Even though we think that Eastern Europe will most likely take precedence over the EU for the delivery of the bulk of Chinese goods for both the Overland Southern Route and the Overland Northern Route, there should still be plenty of Chinese goods left over for several countries within the EU. Let's examine the EU countries most likely to be serviced by both routes:

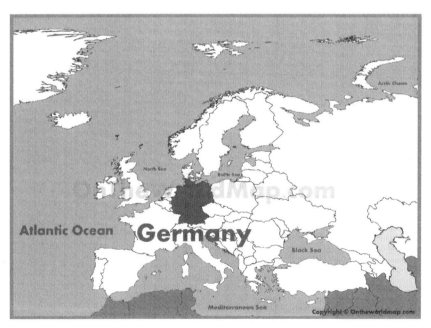

Map of Germany

http://ontheworldmap.com/germany/germany-location-on-the-europe-map.jpg

Germany

Germany will be connected to the Maritime Route by Italian Bullet Trains to Venice. It will be connected to the Southern Overland Route via Turkey and the Northern Overland Route via Russia.

Map of France

http://www.fecielo.com/wp-content/uploads/2009/03/map-of-france.jpg

France

At this point in time, France is not involved in the Belt and Road.

Map of Spain

https://www.pinterest.com/pin/424112489887912189/?lp=true

Spain

At this point in time Spain is not part of the Belt and Road.

Map of Greece

http://casteluzzo.com/wp-content/uploads/2014/07/map-of-greece-980b.png

Map of Italy

Italy

Italy will be a key player in the Maritime Belt and Road.

Germany is on the top of the list for China, but Germany does present a unique EU problem for China. China wants German cars, but trading Saudi Arabian oil for these cars would probably be ill-advised, as it would alienate Russia. That being said, the rest of China's exports are generally low end (phones, clothes, sneakers). This would most likely result in a fairly large deficit for China in exchange of trade with Germany. China could partially offset this deficit with sales of these commodities to Eastern Europe, but would still have to add cash for the import of German cars.

France, Spain, Greece and Italy would be the most likely targets within the EU for China. France has insurance services in the form of AXA to offer Chinese ships on the Maritime Route, Spain offers superior leather products, Greece offers several useful cooking oils, while Italy offers bullet trains to Germany to deliver German cars to Florence or Venice to Chinese ships. Chinese goods will easily cover the costs of these moderately priced imports.

Chapter Four

---✦---

African and Mideast Strategies

With the exception of Saudi Arabia and Djibouti, Chinese trade strategies are fairly straight-forward. China is constantly on the lookout for raw materials in massive quantities at low prices; Africa fits that bill quite nicely. But before we get to the other African and Mideast countries, let's take a look at Saudi Arabia and Djibouti first.

Map of Saudi Arabia

Saudi Arabia

Regardless of whether China can effectively trade in the EU with Saudi Arabian oil, China will still be a massive buyer of Saudi Arabia's oil. China needs oil for China. Russia supplies a large amount of China's oil now, but if the Saudis can beat Russia's price, China will jump right off of the Russian bandwagon. At the very least, negotiating with Saudi Arabia to compete with Russian oil prices will most likely result in a drop of Russian oil prices regardless of whom China buys from. For China, it will be win-win.

And even if China, out of respect for Russia, does not trade in oil with Germany, they still may be able to trade with other countries in the EU. Several EU countries, not in close proximity to Russia, may opt for Maritime Route delivery of Chinese oil procured in Saudi Arabia. And even with a bad scenario of Russia objecting to China trading in oil to ANY EU, China still has three additional options.

China could opt to trade with Eastern European countries; several of which would love to sever their energy dependence on a country they secretly (and sometimes not so secretly) detest. Russia, however, may see this attempt at oil trade in their sphere of influence to be a direct assault on their current market shares. So, a worst-case scenario for China would be a Russian NYET to oil trading in BOTH the EU AND Eastern Europe.

But there are two additional options still open to China even in a worst-case scenario for oil trade in the EU and/or Eastern Europe. China can still sell lots of oil to Turkey, Egypt, several North African countries, several East African Countries, use Djibouti as a storage and refining area, sell to Sri Lanka, India, Indonesia, Singapore, Vietnam, Cambodia. Laos, and Thailand, as well as a few other places.

And the great thing is anything they don't sell, they can always bring back to Beijing for a profit as well.

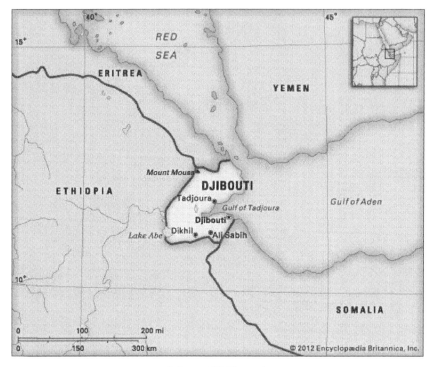

Map of Djibouti

http://media.web.britannica.com/eb-media/70/62270-004-2B18D664.jpg

Djibouti

Djibouti has enormous potential for China. Not only it is a safe haven for Chinese ships about to enter the Red Sea, but it is also a gateway to East Africa. It is a place where China can store massive tons of natural resources for eventual shipment to China. It is also a gateway to trade with several African countries on the East Coast, such as Kenya, and even South Africa.

China will have two, three, or possibly even four major exports to African cities and countries that will redeem millions of tons of valuable raw materials from the virtually endless African supplies of natural resources. China can let Africa have some of the oil they will pick up in Saudi Arabia, they can export Huawei phones by the millions, and Chinese sneakers and clothes by the multi-millions. These markets alone would make the Chinese Maritime Route of the Belt and Road Initiative highly successful.

Africa will be rooting for Russia to exclude China from the EU and Eastern European oil markets so they can take advantage of lower oil prices from Saudi Arabia. Africa desperately needs infrastructure creation, and it will be their natural resources that will pay the bill for that massive undertaking.

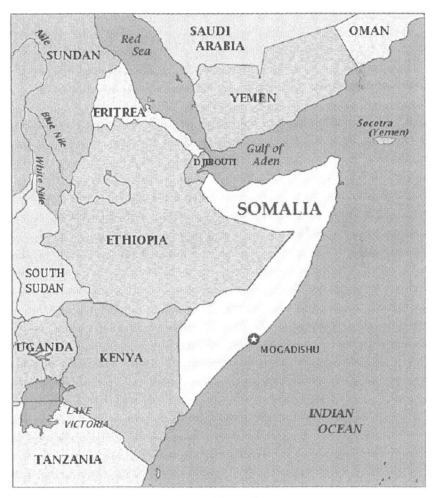

Map of Somalia

https://cofda.wordpress.com

Somalia

Somalia is currently a problem for China and all other countries in the region. Somalian pirates have become, unfortunately, a primary part of the Somalian economy. In order to rid itself of this self-destructive element, Somalia must take two primary steps:

1. It must temporarily place all pirates and even suspected pirates and their families into compounds similar to those that the United States employed at the beginning of World War 2 for Japanese families living on the West Coast. This is primarily for the protection of these people and their families, until Somalia, with the aid of other nations can provide these people with useful jobs and occupations associated with the Belt and Road Initiative.

2. After this temporary camp solution and inclusion into the emerging economic system, Somalia, with the help of its neighbors, must strictly enforce any laws connected with even the most minor piracy activity. Harsh penalties should be exacted on any violators, as acts of piracy will then have to be paid triple compensation by the Somalian government. It will be much more cost-effective to eliminate all pirates by any means necessary.

If Somalia can complete this painful process, it can, once again, be included in the civilized economic world of commerce, protect its national sovereignty (which is currently at risk), and begin to rebuild its cities and coastal areas. If Somalia does not follow this proactive course, it may find itself a conquered country, harshly administered in a fashion much more painful than the above solutions.

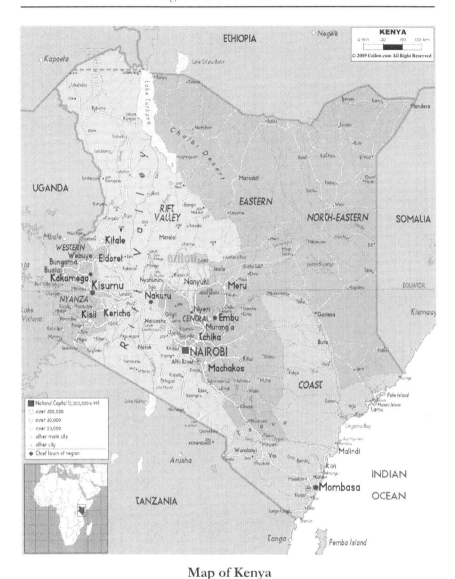

Map of Kenya

https://www.ezilon.com/maps/africa/kenya-maps.html

Kenya

Kenya was originally planned as a stop for the Maritime Belt and Road Route. However, due to the Somalian pirate problem, sailing to Kenya and the city of Mombasa has become more problematic than sailing directly to Djibouti, and having goods shipped from Mombasa to Djibouti instead. This would also save time and money for Chinese ships entering the Red Sea to move onward to the EU.

If Kenya builds bullet trains directly to Djibouti, their shipping problems should be minimized, and they can still be a part of the Maritime Belt and Road Initiative. It may behoove China to assist Kenya in this effort, as it will reduce expenses in the long run for China as well.

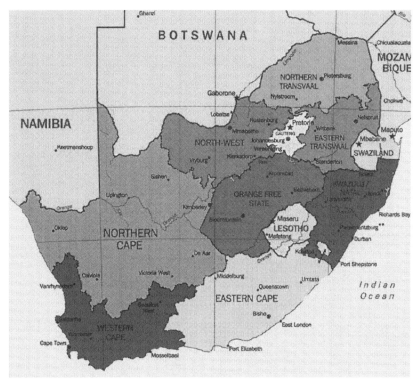

Map of South Africa

South Africa

South Africa could be major export/import market for the Maritime Belt and Road initiative in Africa. As of now, it's location on the Belt and Road is not favorable. Although a goodly distance from Djibouti, it can still participate in this economic venture with the assistance of a high-speed rail system going from South Africa to Kenya and then on to Djibouti. This will take care of two economic problems at the same time by including Kenya along with South Africa as a major importer/exporter along the Maritime Belt and Road route.

South Africa has massive natural resources that China will be very interested in trading for. However, a shipping visit for this exchange would be time-consuming and not be cost-effective. A high-speed rail system connecting South Africa with Djibouti will provide a safer and faster solution than sailing down to South Africa. Items can cheaply be stored in Djibouti as well; especially natural resources. Unless South Africa realizes this solution, they will most likely be left out of the Belt and Road Initiative.

Alternate Maritime Routes

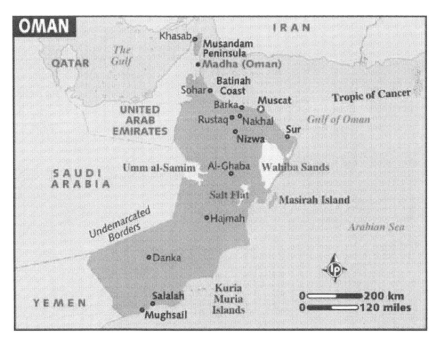

Map of Oman

http://www.eet.ae/web/destination/oman/

Oman

There is only one problem with the Chinese Maritime Route stopping at Oman; it lengthens the time and cost of going directly to Djibouti. China may prefer to have goods from Oman shipped directly to Djibouti for much easier pick-up than by sailing up to Oman and then to Djibouti. If the ship is continuing on to Iraq for oil, then this stop will not be a problem.

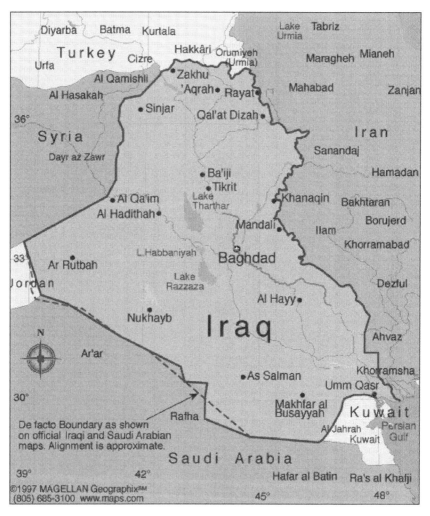

Map of Iraq

https://www.sdvfp.org

Iraq

Stopping at Basra could only mean one thing; that China plans to spend less on Saudi Arabian oi, and may scrap plans to sell oil to EU countries and Africa. Ships making this stop, along with stopping at Oman will have the option of continuing down to Mombasa in Kenya or returning to Asia immediately with the Iraqi oil. They will most likely not be stopping in Djibouti or continuing on the way up through the Red Sea. The cost of doing business in these two places will be less than the cost of doing business with Saudi Arabia, but it will also mean less access to the EU.

The Problem of Easing the Pain of Market Share Loss to the West

It is a pretty good bet that the West will not just idly by while China gobbles up their market shares in Central Asia, the Mideast, Africa, and the EU. Western countries with substantial holdings and market share in each of these critical markets will fight tooth and nail to keep what they have, and to even expand their markets, regardless of the Belt and Road. There will a load of potentially disgruntled countries on this list: The United States, all of South America, Canada, Western Africa, Australia, Japan, India, South Korea, and Taiwan, just to name most of them. And Russia will most likely not be a major part of the Maritime Belt and Road route as well.

The United States will intentionally be left out of the Belt and Road Initiative; all three schemes. The US is handling this news quite calmly for now. It is hoping the Belt and Road will fail; or at the very least not be completely successful. This might happen, and then again, it might not. It is the latter scenario that the US might want to consider; a Plan B, so to speak. They really do not have one at this point of time in 2019.

The US has substantial market shares in several countries within the EU, Africa, and the Mideast. It only has minimal investments in Central Asia. However, losing market share in those EU countries, Africa and the Mideast would be enough to take a painful chunk of American market share out of the market and into the hands of China.

China understands the West will be upset by the economic events that will most likely follow even a moderate success of the Belt and Road. They are prepared to make some trade concessions to the West and individual countries to soothe those countries about the losses of market share they will face. Some of these countries that will lose market share will have only themselves to blame. They possibly could have dodged the Chinese bullet with some aggressive and proactive economic actions, but most will not be proactive; including the United States.

US and Western Resentment, and the Possibility of Retaliation by Japan, Australia, South America, Canada, and South Korea.

So how will the US and the West respond when the writing on the wall becomes painfully apparent? There is an old Western saying "We can all stick together, or we can hang separately" (paraphrase). Right now, Western countries, led by the US, are hanging separately. Sooner or later, they will come to the conclusion that it might be a good idea to formulate, at a minimum, some strategic partnerships, if not a proactive organization that would bring a Western Belt and Road into play to defend itself against China.

There are plenty of candidates for an organization of this type; Japan, Australia, South America, Canada, South Korea, Taiwan, and the Philippines. Individually, these countries would struggle to deflect the loss of market share to China, but together, they would be a formidable association, if they cooperate. They may even increase their market shares with cooperation. At this point in time, however, there is no such cooperation. Problems for each of these countries is as follows:

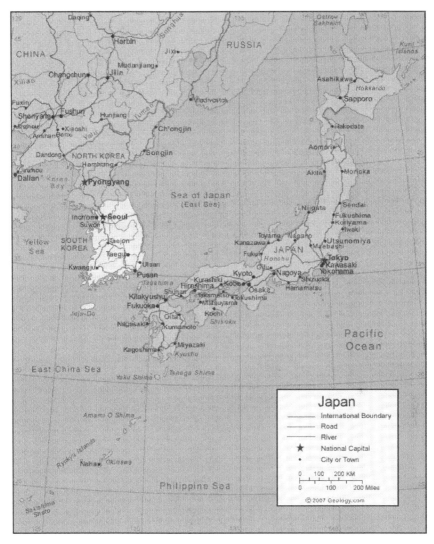

Map of Japan

https://geology.com/world/japan-satellite-image.shtml

Japan

Japan is one of China's major competitors in Asia. China still resents Japan for World War 2. However, China is also Japan's number one trading partner for imports; It imports more motorcycles and cars than any other country. So Japan has to walk a careful line not to offend China too much and jeopardize those substantial markets. The problem, however, is that Japan is completely out of all three variations of the Chinese Belt and Road maps.

How will Japan react to this dilemma? They have a few options; since they have a superior navy. They can partner with regional countries left out of the Belt and Road such as Australia, The Philippines, South Korea, India, and others. As the best navy in the region, they would be a prime mover for an alternative to the Chinese Belt and Road.

Another option for Japan is to partner with the US, but this would be more problematic that making regional agreements or partnerships. The USA would represent a major shift in commerce trade within the Asian theater. The US is also a competitor of the US in several markets, including motorcycles and cars, two staples of the Japanese economy. Initially, Japan may want to limit US participation in any Western Belt and Road creations.

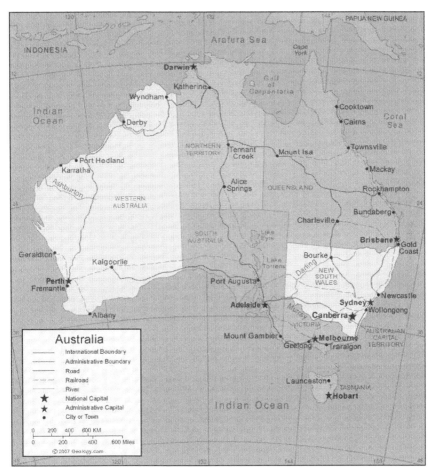

Map of Australia

https://geology.com/world/australia-map.gif

Australia

Australia suffers from problems of geographic location. This fact, plus their close association with the United States, makes them a highly unlikely active participant in the Chinese Belt and Road schemes. Australia has a few options they might want to pursue, however.

First and foremost, since Indonesia is on the way for the Chinese Maritime Belt and Road, it might behoove Australia to create a limited partnership with Indonesia for the purposes of being included in the Chinese route. Indonesia might not jeopardize its relationship with China to allow Australia access. However, even if Australia is unable to partner actively with Indonesia, they will still have a few other options.

Partnering with Japan is not out of the question. This would mean the creation of a new Western Belt and Road scheme separate from China. Australia would probably not partner with Japan alone; a loose association of The Philippines, South Korea, Japan, and India could be possible. Participation of the US might increase or decrease the chance of this association forming. Japan will not be worried about what China thinks.

Partnering with the US is another possibility, but the US is not part of Asia, and partnering only with the US might be perceived as a Western intrusion into Asia. Other partners within the Asian Theater would have to be included, and the title of the association would probably not include the word "Western".

Map of South America

South America

South America has almost no choice for Belt and Road options; they will almost certainly go along with the United States, whether or not the US is proactive or reactive (taking a wait and see position).

Several countries in both Central and South America will be approaching this problem in different ways.

Brazil is the country closest to Africa and any Maritime route that might connect Brazil with West Africa. Although this would be an arduous and time-consuming journey for Chinese ships, it might behoove both parties to cooperate in this venture. China sorely needs the wood from Brazilian rain forests, and Brazil needs Chinese sneakers, clothes and money.

If Brazil cannot partner with China, South Africa might afford them an opportunity, but that partnership would be extremely limiting. More than likely, Brazil will go along with the US and any scheme that the US might concoct. If the United States is reactive or inactive, Brazil will most likely follow suit.

Argentina is another South American country that could profit from trade along the Belt and Road. However, they are not in a very good geographic position to do so. Argentina is famed for its beef, a commodity which China needs, but a recent scandal involving Argentinian beef in the China market, and its subsequent recall, has resulted is diminishing orders for Argentinian beef. This problem, in time, should begin to dissipate, however. Argentina, like Brazil, will probably go along with any US scheme, whether it be reactive, or proactive.

Other Central American and South American countries will have a minimal impact on any of the Chinese Belt and Road schemes. However, Mexico could become a more important player in the future, if the US takes a more proactive approach to establishing a Western Belt and Road.

The Doomsday Retaliation Scenario for the Belt and Road

Then there is a worst-case scenario for China. That would be the defection of Russia to the West and/or the United States or an association including the United States. Although, at this point in time, that likelihood is minimal, such an event would absolutely devasting to China on two levels. Russia would only take such an action if it felt China was not keeping its commitment to the Northern Bell and Road or if Chinese merchants, with or without the knowledge of Beijing and the CPC tried selling Saudi Arabian oil to countries within the EU and Eastern Europe, two staples of Russian exports.

How would the Russians retaliate? Brutally. They would negotiate with the US to create a Russia-US high speed rail system that would easily cross into Alaska and then go down the West Coast to major cities. This move would be devastating to the Chinese Belt and Road routes, and would damage the Chinese economy to a substantial percentage as well. China will do whatever it can to prevent Russia from even considering this type of reaction. They will be very flexible in their dealings with Russia.

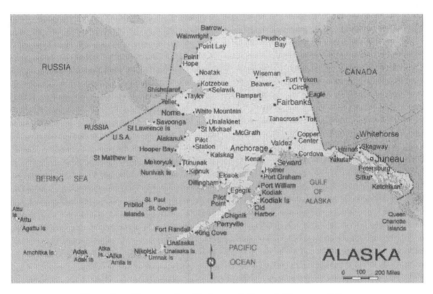

Russian Target for Belt and Road Competition

https://i.pinimg.com/
originals/50/8d/66/508d66e8a604e0c52219e485ac7d6995.jpg

Map of Chinese Nightmare: Siberian-Alaska Pipeline and Bullet Trains to West Coast of US

This could be one of China's worst-case scenarios in the event Russia is not satisfied with their piece of the Belt and Road Initiative.

This scenario would virtually eliminate the need of Saudi Arabian oil in the US, and have negative repercussions in both Saudi Arabia and its partner in oil, China. It would negatively impact the Belt and Road in Asia as well. Although this is still a remote possibility, China must give careful consideration to Russia as a potential competitor as well as a partner.

Beijing Decisions

There are several issues that Beijing must consider in the future development of Belt and Road options: whether the Southern Overland route will primarily begin in Beijing, or whether it will begin in Xian. A second issue will be Beijing's dependence on Tianjin. We will examine both issues in detail. There are additional issues as well.

Xian or Beijing?

Geographically speaking, a line connecting Xian to Urumqi and then Westward to Turkey would seem to be the most logical and cost-effective solution to the Southern Overland Route. There is just one problem with this solution; the base of power in China is not in Xian, but in Beijing. Beijing politicians and businessmen do not want to play second fiddle to a mid-tier city like Xian. Xian may be fine for tourism, but when it comes to massive profits from investments on the Southern Overland Route, Beijing is in a much better position to make deals.

Xian is much closer, and the cost of building infrastructure for the Southern Overland Route would be much cheaper than building a connection to Beijing. But cost and time are not the overriding factors here. Beijing will have its way; Xian will have little to say about that. So, when the major appropriations for the Southern Belt and Road Route are distributed, Beijing's construction will most likely come first.

This is not to say that Xian will be completely left out of the picture. They will also receive funding for infrastructure in the form of bullet trains for a connection between Xian and Urumqi. However, those appropriations will most likely come after the completion of the Beijing to Urumqi infrastructure. It is possible that both cities will have construction at the same time, but it is much more likely that the Beijing-Urumqi connection will be completed first. This has important economic ramifications for both Xian and Beijing.

First and foremost, when the Beijing connection to Urumqi is completed, Beijing will have the opportunity of being first to market. This is an enormous economic advantage. First to market means once Beijing gets to Urumqi, they will be able to claim all the best deals in banking, insurance, export/import, and other deals involving, not only Beijing and Urumqi, but all the countries along the Southern Belt and Road Initiative.

Xian will have to be content just to have a small piece of the pie, and the leftovers in Urumqi (mostly deals involving Muslim populations. Xian, however, will have one small advantage over Beijing. It has a larger Muslim population, since they are located in Central China, than Beijing has. This will serve them well for making deals within several of the predominantly Muslim countries within Central Asia that are along the Southern Overland Route.

Han Chinese are not as comfortable as Muslim Chinese when it comes to working in the countries along the Southern Overland Route. Countries including Kazakhstan, Uzbekistan, Pakistan, Turkmenistan, Iran and Turkey have predominantly Muslim populations. This situation will benefit Urumqi enormously, because there has been economic unrest in Urumqi in recent years. This problem should evaporate, if Urumqi has a sharp increase in employment within Central Asia.

In the final analysis, Beijing will call all the shots. They will take precedence over Xian, Urumqi, the wishes of their partners in the Muslim countries, and over any other objections. Beijing comes first, and everything else comes second.

The Beijing- Tianjin Formula

Beijing will be extremely dependent on Tianjin for Maritime Route commerce. Beijing has no water outlets to the East Coast; it is a landlocked city. However, it is only 30 minutes away by bullet train to Tianjin. This means that Beijing can both send and receive massive shipments to be loaded and unloaded in Tianjin in a matter of a few hours. This should prove to be fruitful for both cities. Make no mistake, however, Beijing will be in full control of all aspects of shipping between both cities and every detail about the destination of all goods. Tianjin will get exactly what Beijing wants to give them.

Tianjin will also be used for storage of goods that will either be shipped in the future, or for goods that have arrived whose ultimate destination is Beijing at some point in the future. Storage fees in Tianjin will be much cheaper than storage in Beijing. Beijing will garner the lion's share of all sales and purchases made on the Maritime Route. Tianjin will be happy just to have some of the bones that are left over.

Tianjin has few native resources and commodities it can trade within the Maritime Route, while Beijing will have an array of materials available for export. Consequently, almost all the goods stored at or leaving from Tianjin will be goods that have originated in Beijing. When it comes to importing, the same situation will take place; Beijing will be importing everything under the sun because it has the money to pay for it, while Tianjin will have to be very selective about the imports it is allowed to take in due to a limited budget.

Other Beijing Decisions

Beijing will be making several other major decisions about all three routes of the Belt and Road Initiative. Within the Maritime Route, it will have to decide the places that will be used for storage. Candidates will include: Tianjin, Shanghai, Ningbo, Fuzhou, Quanzhou, Xiamen, Hainan, Macau, Shenzhen, Guangzhou, and Hong Kong, among others. These decisions will be based on cost of time and distance, and the materials that will be included in the storage and transport.

There will be three types of trips planned for Chinese ships; short trips within the East and South Coast of China that will pick up items stored at various Eastern and Southern cities, Moderately long trips that will stop at Hong Kong, Hainan, Viet Nam, Singapore,

Indonesia, Sri Lanka, possibly some Indian cities, and possibly some Mideastern cities. And finally, there will be the long-haul trips that will go on to Djibouti from Sri Lanka and up the Red Sea corridor. These trips will include stops in the EU or Eastern Europe.

Oil from Saudi Arabia will most likely come back to China (and most likely to Beijing), oil from Oman and UAE can also be sent to China and Beijing, but can also be distributed to partners in Africa and Southeast Asia, as well as Oceania. Ships leaving Tianjin may be leaving with an empty hold if they are bound for Saudi Arabia. This serves two purposes. They are far less likely to be raided by Somalian pirates if they have nothing in their holds going to Saudi Arabia, and secondly, they will be able to fill up the entire ship with Saudi Arabian oil.

However, they will most likely be prohibited by Russia to sell this oil within the EU or Eastern Europe; those are strictly Russian markets. China, however, can still drop off this oil at Egypt for distribution throughout Africa. They can then take their empty holds and proceed to Florence or Venice to pick up bullet train shipments from Germany of luxury German cars. They will then have the option to sell some of these cars on the way back to China and Tianjin (Tianjin will also take a few of these cars as compensation).

The scheme to buy Saudi oil for storage in Egypt and to buy luxury German cars is heavily tilted toward an import-heavy strategy that will require a great deal of cash outlay to put into play. Chinese goods such as Huawei, sneakers, and clothes will not be part of this strategy, and, consequently, not be able to reduce the cash outlay for these endeavors. Other Chinese ships will leave Tianjin fully packed with these Chinese goods, and trade all alond the Maritime Route, creating a cash reserve that they can use once they arrive at Saudi Arabia. Other ships will not stop at Saudi Arabia, and sail right on to the EU and Eastern Europe to continue selling Chinese goods. Then, on the way back, they may pick up oil from Saudi Arabia to sell to Africa, India or partners in Oceania. Anything left over can be stored in Tianjin or another Chinese port.

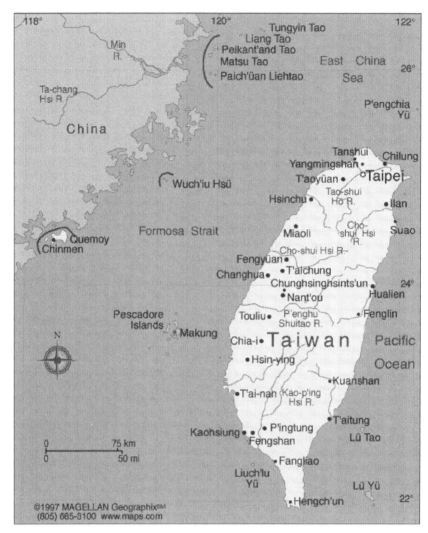

Map of Taiwan

http://econintersect.com/b2evolution/blog1.php/2011/01/28/
taiwan-lowest-tax-burden-in-the-world

The Taiwan Decision

Beijing will also have to decide on what to do with Taiwan. They have clearly indicated that Taiwan cannot participate in the

Belt and Road Initiative unless it is under the complete control of mainland China. Despite that directive, there are several Chinese cities that can benefit from trade with Taiwan within the Maritime Belt and Road scheme. Ironically enough, Beijing is one of those cities. Beijing companies would love to trade Taiwan electronic and tech materials in Africa and the Mideast, but must stick to the policy it has created for Taiwan's inclusion.

Elements of the KMT government still remain in Taiwan, and are adamant about caving in to mainland China demands for Belt and Road inclusion. If the two sides can find some common ground, they could both benefit financially. But there are other cities that would like to make a stop in Taiwan as well. One of them would be Tianjin, which would be carrying goods from Beijing. More than likely Tianjin, would not jeopardize its relationship with Beijing by trying to trade with Taiwan on its own.

However, the further away we get from Beijing, the less influence it has on economic policies. Shanghai undoubtedly will want to trade with Taiwan for Belt and Road materials, and will seek every loophole and avenue of reconciliation it can to achieve that goal. Ningbo will do the same. Shanghai and Ningbo must always follow Beijing policy first, however.

Fuzhou, Quanzhou, and Xiamen are in a bit of a different situation. They are so close to the Taiwan mainland that several trade transactions between the mainland and Taiwan in these cities will be virtually impossible to contain. Massive trading between the cities already takes place with little or no close monitoring by the mainland. What would keep all three cities from trading in goods being prepared for shipment to the Maritime Belt and Road? There is no doubt that some transactions will take place with or without Beijing approval.

There is also the issue of allowing or not allowing Taiwan shipping to dock in Hainan, Hong Kong and Macau. Will Beijing prohibit all shipping from Taiwan in these ports, or just selected ships from Taiwan? Or will they have a policy of all-inclusive shipping to be allowed in these ports from Taiwan? Beijing will have to decide how much, if any Taiwan shipping will be allowed in these ports.

One other issue will be countries who trade with Taiwan who are on the path of the Belt and Road. These countries, especially if they are official members of the Maritime Belt and Road plan might be fearful of losing their standing within the Belt and Road hierarchy. They will most likely avoid trading with Taiwan, unless they have explicit approval from Beijing.

Chapter Five

---🔱---

Problems of Exclusion
and Alternatives

India has a few problems with the Chinese version of the Maritime Belt and Road. The primary problem is that the current version of the Maritime Route only has Sri Lanka as a stop for Chinese trading vessels on their way to Djibouti. All other stops in India would tack on several hundreds of miles of navigation and several additional days to the trip. This would increase the base cost of the trip. It is far more efficient for these ships to pick up Indian goods in Sri Lanka, on the way to Djibouti.

But several cities in India will have great difficulty getting their goods to Sri Lanka, and it will reduce their net profits as well. Will India be satisfied with being marginalized by China to have all their goods go through Sri Lanka. To be sure, there will be exceptions and trips to Indian cities, but these will most likely be regional, and not include stops at Djibouti and the EU going up the Red Sea.

India may decide that this situation is not acceptable. They may partner with Japan, Australia, the United States or other countries to offset the effects of the Chinese Maritime Route. After all, India is an economic competitor of China, and needs to maintain their market shares in the region. They would like to be included in the Chinese Maritime Route, but as it currently is designed, the route does not afford major Indian cities inclusion. This may be by design, as China realizes that India is a competitor within the region for market share.

Major cities like Calcutta, Madras, and New Delhi will need more access than just Sri Lanka. The Indian government will be forced to seek alliances with alternative countries to create an additional scheme for the region that is more advantageous to India. Cooperating with the US for a Western Belt and Road scheme may be in the best interests of the country, and good for the US as well.

The Southeast Asian Problem; Regional Inclusion

Under the current mode of the Chinese Maritime Route, Vietnam is well-represented. However, Laos, Cambodia and Thailand are not. These countries will want to participate in a more active role within the Belt and Road. There are major cities in all three of these countries that will have to send their goods to Ho Chi Minh City or Haiphong in order to participate at this time. Ultimately, this will not be adequate for the needs of one or more of these countries.

The primary problem of all three of these countries, outside of Vietnam, is that they do not have convenient port access on the water for trade. Only Vietnam is conveniently located for foreign visits by water. The other three Southeast Asian countries in this region will be faced with some tough choices.

Thailand has had a great deal of intercourse with the West. So it can easily forge additional relationships with other countries in addition to China for regional and international trade. It will have to forge new partnerships in both the region and internationally to get full benefit for its products.

Laos has a bit of a problem. They are primarily landlocked, and this does not bode well for cooperation with any other foreign country. They may be satisfied with shipping goods to Haiphong or Ho Chi Minh City, or they might explore opportunities with other partnerships. Regardless of any new partners, the problems of access to Laos will always be present.

Cambodia is close to Thailand and has both river and train connections to Ho Chi Minh City. Cambodia may be content with merely being a secondary partner on the Belt and Road, or it may also seek to create new partnerships. India would seem to be the most likely alternative at this time, but nothing yet is in the works.

How will Singapore, Indonesia, Malaysia and the Philippines get inclusion in the BRI?

In addition to Southeast Asia, several countries on the way to the Red Sea area will be interested in broadening their international commerce market shares as well. Among those countries on the Chinese Maritime Belt and Road path to the Red Sea include: Singapore, Indonesia, Malaysia, and the Philippines. Let us examine each of them.

Map of Singapore

http://maps-asia.blogspot.com/2011/09/singapore-map-political-regional.html

Singapore

Singapore has the greatest of all opportunities within the Maritime Belt and Road. Although it may be sympathetic to the possibility of partnering with Western ventures, it will most likely stay in the Chinese camp because of the myriad of potential profits and industries; banking, insurance, oil refining and other major areas of economic power should put Singapore in a very good position.

However, if Singapore did venture outside of the Chinese Belt and Road, it might partner with Australia, the UK or the US as well as Japan and India. Any or all of these potential partners could increase Singapore market shares in the region. However, Singapore must be careful not to ruin their excellent relationship with China.

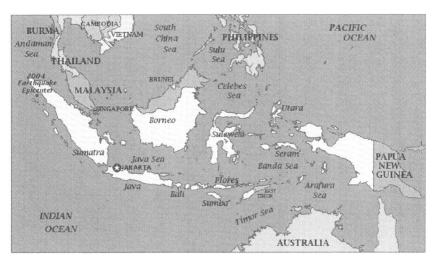

Map of Indonesia

https://sudhirtv.files.wordpress.com/2012/12/map-of-indonesia.gif

Indonesia

Indonesia is critically located in the Maritime Belt and Road. China will be doing a lot of business with Indonesia on several levels. It will be a good idea for China to keep Indonesia happy. Indonesia can very easily partner with Western Countries such as the US and UK, as well as Australia (to which it is in close proximity), Japan and India. Any of these new partnering schemes would be a blow to the Chinese Maritime Route.

Australia desperately needs Indonesia for either inclusion into the Chinese Maritime Route, or for a partner in a non-China partnership. Indonesia will have to balance what can be gained against what could be lost in any future consideration of partnerships with the West or other Asian partners other than China.

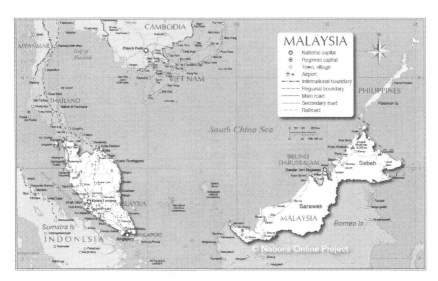

Map of Malaysia

https://ericbrightwell.com

Malaysia

Malaysia is in a fight for market shares with Singapore, Indonesia, and the Philippines. These are the main players within this region. And while they may have friendly relations with all of these countries, a nation's market share is more important than any one relationship within a region. In that respect, Malaysia will want to be included in the Maritime Chinese Belt and Road Initiative.

At this point in time Malaysia's total involvement in the Belt and Road has not been established. It may still be open to further negotiation and deals with mainland China or companies doing business in mainland China. However, at the end of the day, Malaysia may not be happy with a minor share of the action for the region.

An alternative, of course, is to partner with someone other than China for an alternative Belt and Road scheme. Or Malaysia may attempt to keep the Chinese scheme and add additional partnerships to their existing participation. For Malaysia, there will be little to lose if they do not have a major role in the Chinese version. If they can do both, it will be better, but if China protests or threatens exclusion, there is very little to fear from jumping ship, so to speak, from the Chinese model. Malaysia can always do business elsewhere and provide the services that China would have received to China's competition. This is a two-way street, and China may want to keep Malaysia happy with their share of the pie.

Map of the Philippines

The Philippines

The Philippines is an interesting study. While their sphere of influence is solidly in Asia, they have strong ties to the West via Japan and the United States, as well as Australia. It would not take too much of a cold shoulder from China to push this country into an active alliance for an alternative Belt and Road for Western Allies, which would include South Korea as well. This would be a formidable foe to the Chinese Belt and Road.

Fortunately for China, none of these countries have taken a proactive stance against the Belt and Road Initiative. All of them are taking a wait and see reactive stance, which may or may not be the best approach to the Chinese initiative. The United States is still looked upon as the prime mover in the area along with Japan. If these two countries take definitive action, then the rest will follow. Until then, nothing is likely to inhibit China.

Japan

Japan is a wild card here. It is potentially one of the worst case scenarios for China, unless China handles Japan carefully. Japan will not be a major part of the Chinese Maritime Belt and Road. China knows this and Japan knows this as well. China and Japan are fierce competitors within Asia and Japan is winning the trade war between them at this point. This is because China spends much more money on imports of Japanese cars and motorcycles than Japan spends on Chinese imports.

China is not going to allow Japan any access to major markets within its Maritime Belt and Road schemes; you don't provide ammunition for your competition. Japan will be forced to create an association of its own; not only in the Asian region, but internationally, for trade. This association will include all the currently excluded members from the Chinese Belt and Road, and the Western Hemisphere as well.

Members with minor roles in the Chinese Maritime Belt and Road or other routes will have little to lose by leaving the Chinese agreement and moving to a more prominent role under a new initiative by China's competitors and the West. Unfortunately, this appears to be an unavoidable conflict of economies, with little chance of remediation.

Chapter Six

Will China Be Able to Influence Turkey's and Russia's Final Destinations?

The Northern Overland Route Could Turn Out to be a Battle of Wills

Both the Southern and Northern Overland Routes have several interesting alternatives for final destinations. Also the control of these final destinations will be of paramount importance. In the Southern Overland Route, the final destination will be Turkey, and for the Northern Overland Route, the final destination will be Russia. We will examine both of these end destinations and the array of possibilities that could ensue.

Turkish Decisions

Someone is going to make decisions affecting the final destinations of Chinese goods after they reach Turkey from the Southern Overland Route. Will it be China, Turkey, or a third participant? Or it could be the biggest buyer of the goods? Whoever makes the decision where to send the goods will also be making a large profit from those decisions.

If China makes the decisions, it will go strictly to the highest bidder for their goods. If Russia offers the most, the Chinese will sell to them, if countries within Eastern Europe offer the most, then China will sell to the country within that group that will pay the most, And if any EU countries desire these well-priced products, then if they are willing to pay the highest wholesale price, they will get them.

If Turkey makes the final decisions, then the goods will go where they benefit Turkey the most, not where China will make the most money. Destinations from Turkey that could benefit the Turks would be Russia, where the Turks have an Eastern Orthodox Church connection, and Eastern Europe, which is in close proximity to Turkey. However, since the Southern Overland Route is primarily a Chinese operation, there is a very good chance, in the final analysis, that China will retain control of the goods that arrive in Turkey. The reasoning for this is fairly sound.

If Turkey defies China, or does not cooperate fully with China, they may be shut out of the lucrative Eastern European trade routes altogether if China elects to use the Maritime Route as a primary supplier for their goods. This would hurt the Turkish economy, and Turkish financial leaders will make that crystal clear to its political leaders. Once Turkey is aboard with Chinese strategy, then there will be nothing standing in the way of Beijing as to where those shipments can arrive for their final destination. The same cannot be said, however, for the Northern Overland Route through Russia.

Russian Decisions

Russia will be making the lion's share of decisions affecting the Northern Overland Route of the Chinese Belt and Road Initiative. Most of the infrastructure in this route will be built by Russians, most of the infrastructure will be within the boundaries of Russia, and the end destination of the Northern Overland Route will be Moscow, who will obviously make almost all of the important decisions on the usage of Chinese goods reaching that city. Possible destinations would include Scandinavia, Eastern Europe, and possibly the EU as well as other parts of Russia. Russia will disseminate these materials for its own best interests, and China's interests will come second.

Russia has several considerations for final designation of these Chinese goods. They may want to reinforce old alliances with former members of the Soviet Union, or they may want to take advantage of markets that have a great desire for cheap Chinese goods that have moderate quality. In essence, Russia can become the next Walmart distributor of the 21st century in this part of the world. China has no leverage over Russia as far as the final destination of goods are concerned on this route; there are too many variables out of their control.

Russia will ultimately have to strategize exactly how far they would like to impose their will on China. If Russia is excessive in their demands, the Chinese may decide to abandon the Northern Overland Route completely, thereby cutting off a substantial flow of income for Russia and Eastern European countries. Russia does not want that scenario. However, anything short of that scenario will probably be attempted by the Russians to maintain well over 90% control of the transportation, delivery and sales of goods travelling on the Northern Overland Route. We are betting on the Russians having control of this route.

Exclusion and Alternatives

Turkish and Russian decisions will impact countries that will then have little or no participation in the Chinese Belt and Road models. Which countries will accept their fate, and which will veer to the West and the United States? Let's try to break down each of the countries that will be on the outside looking in.

There is already an impressive list of countries excluded on the Maritime Route; including USA, UK, Japan, Australia, the Philippines, and India. If we add the Southern and Northern Overland Route countries that are excluded, then the list becomes even more impressive: The Netherlands, Belgium, Denmark, Sweden, Norway, Spain, France, and Portugal will almost certainly be out of the loop for the Northern Overland Route and the Southern Overland Route will most likely exclude Pakistan, Oman, UAE, Israel, and Jordan. If we add most of the East African countries to the list, as well as all of North and South America, Latin America and a few other countries, we get a list of over 100 countries that are basically excluded from all three routes of China's Belt and Road Initiative.

If these countries can somehow formulate their own coalitions (and as of this writing the former TPP -transpacific partnership, which the US did not join because of IPP concerns, has now reformulated with new IPP statutes; an act to attract the US to join the new arrangement), they could easily compete or even dominate China in the international markets in Asia and the other continents. But as of this writing, that has not yet happened. The US still remains outside of the reformulated TPP, and remains in a reactive, rather than in a proactive stance toward China's trade policies.

Without the US in any international body for international trade within Asia, China should have the edge. However, if the US finally awakens from its economic slumber and actually joins or leads one of these coalitions, it might spell the end to China's run of prosperity. It will certainly curtail their market shares in any of the Belt and Road Maps.

Internal Turkish and Russian Considerations

Turkey

Turkey has several partners within the region; this provides several economic opportunities for them, but poses several significant considerations as well. The primary supplier of Turkey for oil is Russia for two reasons: It has a large Eastern Orthodox Church population in common with Russia, and it borders Russia to the South. It may occasionally import oil from Saudi Arabia, which is also relatively close by, and has Muslim connections within the country, but it pales in comparison to the Russian imports.

So, to keep Russia happy, Turkey will most likely take a pro-Russia stance on the oil issue. But oil won't be arriving on the Southern Overland Route; it will be Chinese microchips, electrical machinery, and clothes. Turkey will have to decide where they will want to eventually send these Chinese commodities, provided they have the authority to do so. And that authority is not a given. China may request, or even demand, that certain quantities of goods go to certain final destinations that would not be in concordance with Turkey.

For example, let us take the microchips. Many of these microchips are produced in Taiwan and mainland China. They are not of the highest quality, as are German chips, for example, but they are adequate for most machines, and the prices are the lowest in the world. For specialized machines, companies would be well-advised to use German or American chips.

Turkey will want to ship many of these ships to various cities in Turkey, but China may want the chips to go on to Eastern Europe as an incentive for Eastern Europe to also purchase Chinese clothing and shoes. Turkey may not have a "let the chips fall where they may" attitude. They may want the chips for themselves, or for Russia. Or they may want to trade with the EU or Mideast countries. Our guess is that the Chinese will have final say as to where these chips go. However, if China is only concerned about selling the chips (and that is quite possible), they may not care at all where Turkey eventually delivers them, as long as they are paid in advance.

Turkey has to keep a lot of different factions happy. There are the Eastern Orthodox Christians, the Muslims, the Russians to the North, the Greeks to the West who would be delivering to the EU, possibly Italy delivering to the EU via bullet trains, Egypt to the Southwest, Syria (a big trouble spot) to the South, Iran (another big trouble spot) to the South, and Central Asia to the East. Turkey is surrounded by potential friends or potential enemies, depending on your point of view. Those are a lot of variables to worry about, and a lot of people to keep happy.

Russia

Russia has far more problems now dealing with Eastern Europe and the former Soviet Union satellites that it did in the pre-1989 era as the Soviet Union. It can no longer just impose its will on these regions. It must seek to create limited partnerships and goodwill; something it has only had 30 years to master, and so far, Russia has not done a very good job of building up goodwill.

It still tries to settle disputes in these regions with threats and blunt force (Ukraine, Georgia). It objects to these countries joining NATO and the US alliance (for good reason). It has relatively good relations with Turkey, although it is still upset with Turkey being a NATO outpost with nuclear weapon capacities. These objections were central during the Cuban Missiles Crisis and part of the eventual deal. Russian ships with nuclear arms were removed from Cuba in exchange for dismantling nuclear weapons on the border of Russia that were stationed in Northern Turkey.

This dismantling was purely superficial though, in Turkey. The missiles were merely moved back a few hundred miles, and still maintained their capacities to totally annihilate their targets from central Turkey. Unlike South Korea, which is biting at the bit to get rid of their nuclear arsenal of US weapons, Turkey is glad to have them as a deterrent for a Russian invasion of any type.

Russia has a lot of people to pacify; it is the biggest place on earth. Parts of Eastern Russia are further away from Moscow than

Hawaii is from the West Coast of the United States. These people need I-pads, I-phones, Macs, computers, modems, and a host of Microsoft products, but they cannot afford the prices. So they will buy Chinese machines and components instead, which although not as high in quality, are moderately dependable, and certainly the cheapest on the planet.

Not only Western Russia needs these commodities, but Moscow, Saint Petersburg, and other major Western Russian cities need this materials as well. Russia does not have a big middle class like the US and Germany; it only earns around 10k a year. That is still twice as much as the average person in China, however, which is less than 5 k a year, according to several sources. People earning that kind of money need the cheapest items available on the market.

Chapter Seven

------- ✦ -------

Excluded Country Strategies in the Maritime Route

There are several excluded countries from the Chinese Belt and Road Initiative Maritime Route. Major players among them are: Japan, Australia, USA, South Korea, the Philippines, India, New Zealand, UAE, Oman, Pakistan, Switzerland, UK, Northern Africa with the exception of Egypt and Sudan, all of East Africa, all Central Africa, all of South Africa with the exception of Djibouti, Portugal, Spain, France, Belgium, Netherlands, Scandinavia, and all of North and South America. That's a lot of disgruntled business people.

Now most of these countries have astute business people, and several of these countries have the cooperation of their governments to foster multinational businesses within those countries. Conversely, several of these countries do not have a clue about the Maritime Belt and Road Initiative, including some heavy hitters like the US. Fortunately, the US has several astute business people within several multinationals that work with or without the cooperation of the American government. All these companies care about is making profits and paying taxes. They could care less about American governmental international political policies and stances. These companies make their own policies and stances within the legal limits of the American legal system.

The same holds true for several other hundreds of multinational companies located in all the areas of the world which currently are excluded from the Chinese Belt and Road Maritime Route model. They may or may not follow the lead of their country's political stances and policies within the legal system of each country. And why should they? Political systems in each country are rarely, if ever, set up for maximizing economic benefit for any one or group of multinational companies within that country. They are set up to maintain power for the political party or parties that happen to be currently in power. In other words, political structures change when political leaders change, but multinationals remain constant. Let's begin with the most important country shut out of the Maritime Belt and Road; that would be the United States.

United States

The United States is a perfect example of the principles mentioned in the previous section. The US government changes political leaders constantly; so policies are often rolled back, erased or changed from the party that was previously in power. This is fine for the political parties concerned; they must try to regain the power they had lost in the previous election or even several elections. But for multinationals, this is not a strategy that makes economic sense.

Multinationals within the United States are concerned with both internal and external environments for their businesses. They are generally apolitical in nature, because it does not pay to support one party at the expense of alienating the millions of voters in the opposition party. You will never see Coke or Pepsi ever take a political stance or support one particular political candidate. They both straddle the fence as much as possible.

The internal environment is generally of more concern for a multinational than is the external environment; unless there is some type of emergency or economic crisis. Given normal circumstances, multinationals are generally concerned with the bottom line; either making more sales or reducing costs to increase profits. That is why Marketing and Operations Production are important internal variables for all multinationals. One increases sales, and the other reduces costs. A good cost accountant can make you more money than an MBA graduate from Wharton School of Business at Penn, or

Harvard Business School. Someone who can save ten million dollars in cost is just as valuable as someone who makes ten million dollars in sales.

Generally speaking, the US government, their think tanks, and their international experts within the government are not all that savvy when it comes to doing business in Asia; and they are particularly clueless when it comes to doing business on the Belt and Road. The general stance of American governmental institutions in the Asian Theatre is reactive, not proactive. This data was collected from American Consulates in China itself. These are first-person reactions, not second-hand data.

And this generally cautious stance is usually a good idea most of the time. A country like the US has a lot of international responsibilities, and cannot afford to go around half-cocked for military confrontations or economic confrontations; it is generally not good business to do so most of the time.

But this is different.

The Chinese initiative for the Belt and Road is so comprehensive, so massive in scope, that it threatens several US multinational market shares in literally hundreds of American businesses; it is a game-changer; and not since Pearl Harbor has the United States been as clueless to the intent of its economic competitors as the US is in this current situation. President Trump did have a clue, and took action against China to try and even the playing field. But his efforts, although successful to a degree, will only be a thumb in the dyke that is about to break.

Much, much more is needed. A proactive stance must be initiated or several US companies will suffer extensive economic damage in market shares within the Maritime Route. The US will lose market shares in Turkey, all of Central Asia, Eastern Africa, several areas within Oceania, and, in particular, the EU. The market share losses within the EU will be devastating, unless there is a mechanism in place to effectively counter the Chinese Maritime Route for the Belt and Road.

This is not alarmism; it is just pure common sense. If you do not protect your market shares, then your competition will take them away from you; simple business survival of the fittest. Hopefully, an

Asian and EU combine of some type will be created and implemented in time to save these market shares, and possibly even increase them.

Canada

Canada, the staunch ally of the United States, is also out of the Maritime Belt and Road Route. But Canada has an ace up its sleeve. It has massive quantities of oil that it can easily export to the EU at prices below what the Chinese will offer EU countries from oil purchased in Saudi Arabia. Canada might have trouble competing with Saudi Arabia as a primary provider, but as a middle man, China would have to add in its profit margin, and still try to undercut Russia (which will be very difficult to do).

Canada has no need for a middle man, but they still must compete with Russia, who also does not have an oil middle man. Russia has a few advantages; it is on the border of several EU countries, and in close proximity to many others; Canada is further away, but it is not as far away as China, so they could beat the Chinese in the oil game, and take the Silver Medal. China would have to settle for the Bronze, but they can still make money as the third best dealer of oil.

Canada has a natural ally in UK, and the UK has good connections in Hong Kong. The UK also has good connections in the EU, even though they are exiting the EU. These connections could prove to be valuable, if Canada would like to explore the oil market in the EU. UK would be the banking and insurance partners in these deals.

Japan

Japan and India are the two biggest players outside of China in Asia. Neither have been included in the Belt and Road Maritime Route in any significant way. Neither country can afford to settle for the crumbs they will be offered by China. Japan is a major competitor of China in several key markets. China also still holds a strong grudge against Japan for World War Two atrocities that Japan has never apologized for. Of all the countries that have been left out of the Chinese Belt and Road, Japan is the most likely to take proactive economic action.

Japan has already made the Daiyu Islands an issue with China; drawing assistance from the United States, another orphan in the Chinese scheme. Between Japan's powerful navy and the US, with its powerful navy, China has no choice but to tread very carefully in the South China Sea area. But saber-rattling will not be enough.

In addition to military preparedness, both the US and Japan need to take a more proactive economic role in the establishment of an Asian coalition to counter the Chinese Initiative. So far, Japan has been fairly active; trying to unite the region, including other outcasts such as South Korea and Australia to formulate their own league. The US, however, continues to be very cautious and tepid in their response to the Chinese economic threat. Unless the Japanese and India can induce the US into the new organization, it will probably fail to counter the Chinese initiative.

India

India is in the same boat as Japan, although China has thrown a few inducements to India to include them in two vague routes within the Maritime Route. One route has the inclusion of Calcutta in the Maritime Route; but this appears to be a highly unlikely development. If a Chinese ship sails from Singapore or Indonesia to Djibouti, it would most likely pass by Sri Lanka, not go 1000 miles out its way to Calcutta. Forcing India to send all of its goods to Sri Lanka to be included in the Chinese Maritime Belt and Road might not be too favorable for India. They would be spending millions of shipping dollars and travelling an extra thousand miles just to be part of the action.

To Include Calcutta and other large Indian cities, Japan and the US would almost certainly have to be involved. Possibly the UK, with its experience with India, might be involved as well. These are all countries that are currently on the outside looking in for the Belt and Road. So what is the likelihood that the UK, the US, Japan, India, Australia, and South Korea will all unite to overcome the Chinese threat? Unfortunately, the prognosis is not too good. It would take a level of cooperation that all of these countries have not yet achieved. China is banking on the lack of cooperation among these countries, and it appears to be a pretty safe bet.

Australia

Australia is an unusual case. They are located close to China, but geographically, they are too far West of China to take advantage of their proximity. Australia will have to depend on the third-party services of Indonesia or Singapore in order to become more actively involved in the Belt and Road. Ideologically, Australia is closer to UK and the US, but economics almost always trumps ideology in the long run, and Australia will most likely go along with the Chinese scheme, unless the unlikely association of Japan, the US, India and others takes place.

Australia has a lot to bring to the table. They have enormous natural resources and a small population; two advantages that China does not enjoy. China and Australia already have several deals in the works. But it still appears as if Indonesia and/or Singapore will have to come to the rescue of Australia, if they want to expand their role in the Belt and Road.

South Korea

South Korea does not really have a lot of cards to play in this global economic game. It is obviously far superior to North Korea economically, and for that reason, a much more attractive trading partner for China. However, South Korea suffers from the same problem that Australia suffers from; it is in the opposite general direction of the Chinese Belt and Road Route.

One of the few options for the South Koreans, if they want to convince the Chinese that trade is very important to them, is to loosen their ties with the United States; especially when it comes to nuclear weapons. China will demand that South Korea denuclearize the Korean Peninsula for two very good reasons: one, it will get rid of US weapons in South Korea, and two, it will provide a rationale for China to talk down the leader of North Korea from maintaining nuclear weapons in that country. The literal fallout from a Korean War, would damage the Chinese economy, and they will do anything to prevent that from happening.

The Philippines

The Philippines have the potential to become players in the Belt and Road. They are just off the primary path, they have several marketable products, and they have several million Chinese expatriates living in their islands. On the negative side, they currently are having a dispute with China over the South China Sea, they are too closely aligned with the United States, the primary economic competitor of China, and they still have problems with Muslim insurgents on one of their islands. This type of instability generally keeps Chinese businessmen from investing too heavily in any ventures within those areas.

However, there could be a silver lining here, and a win-win for both the Philippines and China. If the Philippine government and the Chinese business community can recruit the local Muslim population to work on the Southern Overland Route that primarily goes through Muslim countries, then the Philippines can finally solve one of their greatest domestic problems, and make money for their citizens at the same time to help their economy. The key here is how the Chinese handle Urumqi, and if the Muslim citizens of that area prosper from the Southern Overland Route. China will then be able to use that success to convince the Philippines to do the same.

If, however, the Chinese fail to solve their Muslim Urumqi problem, then they will never be able to sell that same idea to other countries like the Philippines.

The UAE, Oman, and Pakistan

We have included three Arab Peninsula nations in the same analysis because they all have similar problems within the scope of the Chinese Belt and Road Initiative Maritime Route. Let's begin with the UAE. The UAE has oil, just like Saudi Arabia, but they have one severe problem; location, location, location. They are off the beaten path of the Maritime Route, and so they are not an attractive alternative to Saudi Arabia, which is right on the Red Sea corridor on the way to the EU.

Some Chinese businessmen, however, will be intrigued by the possibility of not continuing on to the EU. They might just want to pick up oil from the UAE (which is closer to China than Saudi Arabia), and then take it back to Singapore to refine it at the most modern refinery in Asia. They could then sell the oil to Southeast Asia, Oceania, and various cities in China. They would also save time and distance for their ships sailing up the Red Sea. This strategy would only be attractive to businessmen having no intention of selling their goods to the EU.

The same strategy would hold true for Oman, but not for Pakistan. Pakistan has their own set of problems due to their unique location. They are primarily a landlocked country, and this does not bode well for a Maritime Route Plan. To add to the problem, they are not directly on the way to Iran and Turkey for the Southern Overland Route, so they will most likely be left out of that picture as well. The only alternative for Pakistan to participate in either the Maritime Route or the Southern Overland Route is the same approach the Philippines will be taking; except that Pakistan has a much larger work pool force to choose from for working in Muslim countries. That is their best chance for inclusion.

The North African Nations

With the exception of Egypt, North Africa will pretty much be left out the Maritime Route. Countries like Libya and Algeria are not in the current scheme, but could become active as recruiting areas for the necessary Muslim workers the Chinese will need for the Southern Overland Route. The only problem here is that Pakistan and the Philippines are closer in proximity to China, as well as Urumqi, for recruiting these types of workers.

So the current prognosis is that these countries will most likely still be left out of the picture, and they have little chance of aligning themselves with Western Powers like the UK, USA, and Canada, which have distrust for Muslim countries. The only ray of hope for these countries is that the Western Powers will need Muslim workers to compete with the Muslim workers recruited by the Chinese for the Southern Overland Route. This outcome only has a slight chance of taking place; a bit under 25%, so things do not look too bright for these countries.

The Central African Nations

The Central African nations such as the Congo and others have two main problems to deal with; they are virtually landlocked, and they are not directly on the way to the Chinese Maritime Route. The only likely alternatives for these countries is to send their goods directly to Djibouti to be picked up by Chinese ships on their way up to the Red Sea.

The South African Nations

The South African nations, and South Africa in particular, are nowhere near the Chinese Maritime Route, however, South Africa has a few precious trade items coveted by the Chinese; diamonds and gold. A deviation of over a total of 1000 nautical miles would result in a trip to South Africa and others near them, so it is not likely Chinese businessmen will be able to make sufficient profits by taking the opposite direction of most business that will be conducted on the Maritime Route. This condition is likely to push South Africa closer to the Western Bloc.

The West African Nations

The West African nations are currently almost completely out of the picture for any of the Chinese trading routes, but that does not mean that West Africa does not have alternatives. They will most likely be pushed into the Western camp, which includes the United States and South America. There are opportunities for all of these countries to cooperate and create their own trade routes to compete with China, but will they take the necessary proactive action that would be necessary to do so? The betting here is that they will not; particularly the United States.

Excluded EU Countries

Excluded EU countries are numerous; they include the UK, Portugal, France, Belgium, Spain, Switzerland, Scandinavia, and all of South America, as well as the Caribbean and Central America. The UK has the best chance of all these countries and areas to become heavily involved in Belt and Road activities.

Although they are currently mildly excluded, with a little effort, they can easily take the forefront of Western Nations in NATO (and most NATO nations are excluded and become a big player in the Belt and Road. The English have two major tools to work with; their banking within HSBC, which has several hundred offices within China and India, and their insurance expertise within Prudential, one of the world's leading insurance companies for capital ventures.

Even Chinese businessmen will be looking to do business with the UK in either one or both of these essential services, as China Life and Ping An do not have the track record that Prudential, or even AXA of France, possesses. In addition, the UK has tons of experience from their colonial periods in dealing with Asia. They are an excellent bet to overcome their original exclusion.

Portugal is another good bet. Portugal is a clever country with lots of colonial experience as well with Africa. They might easily become included in deals involving Djibouti, and send their own fleet of ships to deal with that area of Africa. Their only concern, of course, will be the Somalian pirates.

France and Belgium are pretty much in the same boat. They will have to depend on their old colonial connections in Africa as well to try and do the same strategy that Portugal will employ. Also, France has some intercourse with UK and Germany, the latter slated to be a big player in the Belt and Road.

Switzerland's newest financial foe will now be Singapore. Singapore will have almost all the inside tracks to financing and deal-making within the Maritime Route, but that situation might change if there is a successful Northern Overland Route that goes through

Russia and Germany. Switzerland would obviously be the choice over Singapore in that situation.

Scandinavia has an unusual situation. They will initially be left out of the Belt and Road routes for the Maritime and Southern Land Route, but could be a hot commodity if there is a successful completion of the Northern Overland Route. There are still a lot of obstacles, however, for the completion of a successful Northern Overland Route.

Spain has a large Muslim community and close ties to Africa. They might fit in as a recruitment center for Muslim workers in the Southern Overland Route, but it is more likely those workers will be recruited from Urumqi or the Philippines. Spain will have to rely on their ties to African countries doing business on the Belt and Road.

South American and Central American Strategies

And finally, we have the massive amount of countries within the South American and Central American sector that are currently out of the Chinese Belt and Road plans. Even Brazil, which is officially a trading partner of China under BRIC, will have the same fate as all the other BRIC members; exclusion from the Maritime Route. Russia and India are also excluded, so the BRIC coalition that includes Brazil would seem to be doomed in the future, if all three countries are not included in the Maritime Route.

The prospects for other countries in South and Central America are not better than Brazil, with the possible exception of Argentina, which has a very large beef supply, a commodity that China badly needs. But even if Argentina gets into the Maritime Belt and Road, it will still be geographically way out of the picture, even with a partnership with West African nations.

Summation

After a very short period of success by China in the Maritime Belt and Road, it will become painfully clear to the West that they have literally missed the boat, By that time, of course, it will be much too late for most Western countries to economically respond. China will have had the First-To-Market advantage (that is like landing the first good punch in a fight). In addition, the pain for the West will only increase with Chinese ventures into both the Southern and Northern Overland Routes, exacerbating the market share losses the West is almost sure to endure from the Maritime Route.

Will the West respond in time to save themselves? Will the Wait and See Strategy of the US backfire? Why not hedge bets on the future? Why not create useful regional partnerships to avoid potentially devastating market share losses? Allowing your economic competition to take the initiative is usually not a good idea. If this were a hot war instead of an economic war, the US would have responded long ago. Will they be able to recover lost market share? Will American MBA students finally get a clue about how to do business in Asia and China? Only time will tell.

Paul Eberle, Phd
Arthur H Tafero, Phd

Made in the USA
Monee, IL
13 May 2020